A Time of Change

A Time of Change

Akashic Guidance
for Spiritual Transformation

Aingeal Rose O'Grady

Wild Flower Press
P.O. Box 1429
Columbus, NC 28722

Series Information
First in the Honest-To-God Series

Library of Congress Cataloging-in-Publication Data
O'Grady, Aingeal Rose, 1953-
A time of change : Akashic guidance for spiritual transformation /
Aingeal Rose O'Grady.
    p. cm.
Includes bibliographical references (p. 179).
ISBN 978-0-926524-72-9 (alk. paper)
1. Akashic records. I. Title.
BF1045.A44O37 2013
133.9'3--dc23
2012030227

Cover and interior Artwork: AHONU Kevin O'Grady
Manuscript Editor: Brian L. Crissey
Manuscript Designer: Pamela Meyer

Printed in the United States of America.

Address all inquiries to:
Wild Flower Press
an imprint of Granite Publishing
P.O. Box 1429
Columbus, NC 28722

http://granite-planet.net

DEDICATION

I dedicate this book to the Truth
that forever lives within each of us,
waiting patiently to be remembered and awakened.
To the heart, mind, soul and spirit of which we are all made,
to the divine reasoning with which we can understand.
Let your True Selves come forth in their shining radiance
of Everlasting Love.
Peace, peace, eternal peace.

ACKNOWLEDGEMENTS

It is impossible to write a book alone. Without the continued help, support and encouragement of others you would not be holding this book, *A Time of Change* in your hands. Every book that gets published anywhere demonstrates that we are a collective who has the joy of inter-relating and creating with one another as reflections of God Source, which is also, *ourselves*.

My Beloved husband, AHONU, is the first person to thank for the success of this book. He is responsible for the beautiful cover art as well as all the illustrations presented before each chapter. Without his formatting and organizing of the chapters, I would never have made my deadline! When I was taking breaks, he was tirelessly working. Thank you, AHONU, for your love and support! I love you!

Next I would like to thank my publishers, Pam and Brian Crissey, for their faith in me and in this material. At a time when things on Earth are speeding up and changing so quickly, I am grateful for the opportunity to get this information out to the world.

I would also like to express my deepest gratitude to all the wonderful people who regularly attend my Akashic Group Sessions in person and online across the globe. Without you and your incredible questions, God Source would not have had the opportunity to come forth and educate and inspire us all on such a wide variety of subjects. I love and appreciate you all!

Finally, thanks, Mom and Dad, for giving me life on this planet during this auspicious time, and thank you, my beautiful children, Clayton, Brooke and Janai, for filling my life with love and joy and for giving me my awesome granddaughter, Gracie Rose. You live within me forever!

Aingeal Rose O'Grady
North Carolina, 2012

Table of Contents

Preface

No one can deny that we live in exciting times. Changes are occurring almost daily on every level of our lives. Never in our lifetime have we been witness to a global awakening of this magnitude. Every aspect of life is affected—thoughts are manifesting at a rapid rate for good or ill. Systems are failing and new ways of thinking are starting to make way for a more cooperative and harmonious way of life.

The people are ready. Children are being born with exceptional gifts demonstrating that the human race is changing into a more spiritually evolved species. Neck in neck with that, those involved with the old system of war, greed, corruption, competition and control are trying to enslave us even further. We have been under that thumb for far too long!

To succeed in a new paradigm, we must *all* be willing to change—to choose differently—to be more self-sovereign—to cooperate and share, to *care*. Establishing communities that are self-sustaining on all fronts is an absolute necessity for life to continue to flourish, not just survive.

Where is God Source in all this? *Is* there a God Source? Does *It* have a hand in the orchestration of these changes? Is this Armageddon or Paradise? Are cataclysmic Earth changes a necessary part of these times?

I have been a reader of the Akashic Records for the past 15 years. Akashic comes from "Akasha" which is a Sanskrit word meaning "ether" and implies a spiritual plane or substance where the entire history of Life is recorded and kept. "Akasha" has been described as an ancient Library where each one of us has our own "book" of our many lifetimes and sojourns in Spirit. This "library" has been given the name "the Akashic Records."

Through accessing the Akashic Field, I have been privileged to provide understanding, guidance and comfort to my clients from levels that go far beyond our linear view of life. I too have learned through these readings, and

I certainly have understood there are causes for everything in our lives. Everything *does* make sense—this is the gift of the Akashic Records.

People who have had near death experiences (NDE) report seeing their entire lives flash in front of them on point of death. This is evidence of the Akashic Records, the recording of even the minutest detail of a person's life. Not only are the events of life recorded, but the ***impact*** of those events on ourselves and others is also recorded. The implications of this are a bit mind boggling if you think on it!

What Intelligence is it that would bother to record all the events of life? What would be the purpose? That it matters a great deal is obvious when we see that it is part of the life and death-transition process. Each and every person is presented a "life review," a summary of his or her life, those they've affected and were affected by. Those returning from NDEs report that not only do they "see" all the events of their life; they also *feel* the impact of their choices upon others for good and ill. Progress and learning is observed and noted as well as choices made. Could things have been done in a better way? What victories were obtained? Our progress is observed and measured not by a punishing God, but by *ourselves*. It is *we* who are in our own relationship with ourselves, with our Creator and with one another.

So, what *is* the purpose of Life, ***our*** Lives? What is wanted of us from our Creator's or "Life's" point of view? Why do we keep coming and going? Why do we arrange to meet others again and again with whom we have shared lifetimes before? Are we on missions? Or is our purpose unique to each soul?

Questions such as these were the impetus for me to begin the group Akashic Record sessions. I ventured on this group experiment based on questions my clients were asking of God and the universe. I had plenty of my own questions as well! The groups began in Ireland in 2010 and continue to this day. They have been recorded In Ireland, California, North Carolina, Upstate New York and recently, through webinars online (see http://aingealrose.com).

The book you are now reading contains transcripts of some of those meetings with God Source through the medium of the Akashic Records. This book is the first in a series of books in the ***Honest-to-God*** series. Each one will touch on a variety of topics on spirituality, the world, healing, God, love, miracles, ancient civilizations and more.

Many have asked me *how* I receive the information from the Records. My answer is multi-layered. Once I am in "the Akashic Field," I am in a field of vast information. That information translates itself into beams of color, words, feelings, knowings, and pictures. It is as though the information is "impressed" upon my body so that as I receive the information, I also feel and experience it at the same time.

Many times it all occurs at once, and it is my job to "report" the information to my client or group. Words coming from Source are very deliberate and "in order." By this I mean I must report the information in the sequence it is given, *exactly* as it is given, before the next piece will be shown to me. I also would not use the same choice of words to get a meaning across to the same two people in a private reading. Source understands *how* a person can **receive or hear** the information It wants to impart.

Getting into the Akashic Records is done through an ancient sacred prayer that I was taught many years ago. My teachers told me the prayer was an ancient Mayan prayer that was translated into English. Upon saying the prayer (the first part is said aloud, the remaining two parts are silent), I am immediately in the Akashic Field. Each session ends with a Sacred Prayer as well.

I have decided to leave the transcripts of these group sessions in their original question-and-answer format, just as the sessions were presented and recorded. Since I am not in trance while receiving this information, the discussions are often free-flowing until I receive another clear impression. Therefore, at times, I have included additional information on a particular topic from other sessions, from my own conversations with Source, or from my personal experience. Please note that when I'm telling a personal story, the text is indented so as to distinguish my words from those of Source.

Throughout the transcripts, you will hear me reference "Source" quite often. Source in these contexts is our Prime Creator—the original Intelligence or "God" that is aware of everything and knows everything and everyone. At times I have referred to Source as "They" only because it *feels* to me that Source is not only "Prime," but also "All That Is."

In these sessions, it is Source Itself that talks to us and answers our questions. Although we are visited from time to time by light beings, in these sessions there are no "middle men"—no masters, guides, angels or other intermediary beings.

It is my desire in offering these transcripts to you that you will experience the peace and understanding from God Source that has always been ours to remember.

While I am in the "field" of the Akashic Records, I experience consistent love and peace, as well as a knowing that all is well despite what may be occurring or appearing to the contrary in our world or in our personal lives. It is my hope that you will be inspired and uplifted by these understandings and that your own connection to God Source will be enriched.

With Love,
Aingeal Rose

Explaining the Levels

In this book, we speak with God Source on a wide variety of topics. Since the questions are so wide and varied, the answers cover many levels from the strictly mundane or 3-D perspective, to inter-dimensional levels, and to the deeply spiritual – or "Big Picture." Even so, there are core themes that run through each topic:

- There is a Higher Plan in creation
- We are part of the carrying forward and success of this Plan
- Each one of us shapes our souls and contributes to the Whole.

Throughout the discourse you will hear talk about the Negative Agenda's (NA) plan vs. the Plan of God-Source. This is only to show the contrast between them and to be greater able to discern the myriad of influences present in our world. This contrast also leads us to the realization that these polarities exist within each one of us as our "*split* spirit-soul-mind-brain-body composition." Since our outer world reflects our inner world, it is up to each of us to decide which plan we are energizing and do the necessary clean-up in our self-perceptions to support only God's Plan.

Historically, we have been attempting to serve two masters—our true spirit identity and our fallen earth identity, and it can no longer be done. That we experience continual conflict with these aspects of ourselves is obvious. *(See Chapter 2 "Who are we and why are we here" for more explanation.)*

The only way to offer *all* of humanity (NA included) a collective karmic release is to choose to activate our original spirit self before the fall (*See "Q. What happened to cause the Fall?" on page 12.*) and *only* that. The God within each of us is a way of being and it is applicable across the board regardless of who's doing what in the outer world. Source has made it very clear throughout these transcripts what Its intention for all creation is, and never sways from that.

In response to some questions you will hear Source say it has no opinion, and yet in response to other questions It will appear to have a strong opinion. This occurs when Source desires to get a message across to us of some importance that we can only grasp at our own level of understanding.

Therefore, what may appear as a contradiction is really a deliberate attempt by Source to make a point at the level of understanding of the one asking the question. In these cases, it is important to keep in mind the levels that are being addressed in response to questions.

Source has also clarified the Spirit-individuated spirit-soul-mind-brain-body levels by defining each in this way:

Spirit—the *essence* of which all life is created, which is perfect in its *composition or "order,"* but *not* perfect in its *individuation* into the diversity of life forms. This imperfection could be the result of the splitting off into various life forms, but it is clear that each individuated spirit is on its own journey or evolution back to God realization or "Home."

Individuated spirit—the thinker, the decider and the observer. Because it is individuated, it has experiences and can be injured and traumatized, which affects how it sees and thinks of itself for good or ill. The "self concept" is made at the level of the individuated spirit.

Soul—the *accumulation* or record of an individuated spirit's journey —its successes and challenges. Inherent in this would be the individuated spirit's levels of personal mastery—what it has gained—on its journey to God realization.

Mind—the substance which takes ideas and concepts and formulates them into expressions which appear in what we perceive as "outer reality." True healing cannot occur at the mind level, as it is not the *originator* of concepts—the individuated spirit is.

Brain—the *energetic interface* between the mind and the body. The brain relays messages to the body complex from the conceptual mind field coming from the individuated spirit's concept of itself. This self-concept is formed into messages through the mind field, which relays them to the brain interface. The brain interface then relays these to the body system, which is formed after its kind in chemical, hormonal and cellular composition.

Body—the body is the *matter expression* of the individuated spirit and serves as a vehicle in this dimension for the purpose of experiencing, learning, expressing and affecting the quality of life in this density.

It is easy to see in understanding the cascade effect of this process, that true and permanent healing can only occur from the level of 1) the choices the *individuated spirit* makes and 2) the *willingness* to have God Source Itself assist in the repair and correction of any distortion in identity that the individuated spirit may be carrying in its spirit body. These repairs would naturally see their effects down the levels to the soul, mind, brain and body.

These subjects will be covered in greater detail in Book 2 in this series, *The Nature of Reality*, but are necessary to introduce now.

Questions to the Records
About the Records

Chapter 1

Questions to the Records about the Records

Q. WHAT IS SOURCE'S DEFINITION OF THE AKASHIC RECORDS?

A. Source's definition of the Akashic Records is that it is a field of information like streams of color or spheres of light, and not necessarily language. It is similar to different frequency bands of information which vibrate as different colors or resonate as sounds. It is part of the collective unconscious where everything that ever was or ever will be resides. It is the same as saying that it is the "All That Is." Once something is added to it, it *is*—in other words—it *exists*. Once something exists, it is there in the "Field," and it registers as different colors or frequencies of information.

Q. IF ALL TIME IS SIMULTANEOUS, HOW DOES IT REGISTER SOMETHING AS HAVING "HAPPENED"?

A. Once something has happened, it is there. It doesn't have a distinction with time; it is rather part of the whole, which is timeless. It does not distinguish among past, present, or future—it just *is*.

Q. WHAT'S THE PURPOSE OF THE AKASHIC RECORDS?

A. The purpose of the Akashic Records is for God's pleasure and our pleasure. It is the same as asking "What's the purpose of existence?" because they are one and the same. The Akashic Records are records of existence—of everything that exists, and existence is for God's pleasure.

Q. ARE THE RECORDS OPEN TO ANYONE ALL OF THE TIME OR ARE SOME RECORDS CLOSED OR SEALED?

A. God's information is open to everyone and is free to everyone. There are no Records that are closed. However, if you are not at a certain level of consciousness, there are Records you cannot access or read. Since they are a collection of *frequencies*, your ability to access the memory or the "All That Is" has everything to do with your own state of consciousness.

Q. ARE THERE SPECIFIC "RULES" TO ACCESS THESE RECORDS?

A. There are no rules *per se*, however it is a field of *vibration,* and accessibility has everything to do with your own motives and levels of awareness. So the "rules" are—you can't access "the Field" unless you resonate at its frequency.

Q. ARE THERE SPECIFIC PRAYERS TO ACCESS THE RECORDS, OR WOULD AN INTENTION SUFFICE?

A. There is more than one prayer that can be said, but more than that, it is about your *intention* or your *purpose* for accessing the Records. Anyone with the wrong intentions cannot access higher frequencies. The advantage of certain prayers is that they will uplift you to higher frequencies *temporarily.* Your ability to align yourself to those frequencies will determine how able you are to read the Records. Specific prayers do make a difference.

Q. ARE CERTAIN PEOPLE BETTER ABLE TO ACCESS THE RECORDS THAN OTHERS, AND IF SO, HOW DOES THIS AFFECT THE INFORMATION COMING THROUGH?

A. Yes, certain people are able to access the Records better than others, which affects the *translation* coming through in the down-stepping process. It has to do with an individual's own filters of consciousness—*i.e.* their opinions and belief systems may taint the purity of what they can receive.

You can teach a prayer to anyone, and that prayer can help them reach a certain frequency level, but how *able* that person is to *match* that frequency or down-step the information has a lot to do with their own abilities. The exception to this would be to go into a hypnotic state similar to Edgar Cayce, where the perceptual filters are bypassed and would not be interfering. Keep in mind, however, that with the hypnotic process, the translator could be susceptible to wear and tear on his mind and body if he or she is not *naturally* attuned to certain higher frequencies.

Q. CAN YOU PREDICT THE FUTURE IN THE RECORDS?

A. In the Akashic Records you can see probable futures. By this is meant that there are an infinite number of possibilities or "time lines" that offer future potentials. When we see a "probable future" in the Records, it is showing a possible future outcome if no change is made. However, a "probable future" is not etched in stone—it is only a *potential* based on consciousness at the time the question is being asked.

Q. CAN THE RECORDS BE CHANGED?

A. No, they can only be *added* to. For example, let's say science/technology has discovered a way to go back into the past and change an event. The original event is still recorded as it happened. You can't go back and take something out of existence once it has existed. What you *can* do is create a *new* event in a certain time period, but you are not taking away the old event. You are *adding* to the existing event or time period. This can be done because thought is creative, and in the realm of thought, time, space and distance do not exist.

It is easy to go to an event or time period and create a new scenario with your mind. Because you are thinking it and visualizing it, it is being added to the Field. You have now just created another possible time line with a different outcome in a certain time period. Since in the thought field everything is happening all at once, your visualization is being registered in the "place" or "time" of your intention.

See "Q. Is there a way that people can get into the Akashic Records and change the future of what's going to happen collectively?" on page 82.

Q. CAN YOU ERASE YOUR OWN RECORDS, AND WOULD IT BE DESIRABLE TO DO SO?

A. No, you can't erase your own Records. Nothing is ever lost, but what does go is any *attachment* you may have to an event, time period, experience, person, *etc.* When we talk about erasing the Records, we are talking about erasing the "charge" that's attached to them. It is a way of reconciling your past. Think of it as psychic energy or cords that you may have to certain aspects of your personal history—some might call it "karma."

It is desirable to go back into your own past and make peace with it. It is still recorded as memory, but there are no longer any cords or unforgiven issues. You don't really erase it out of the "Library," but you do erase the *attachment* or anything left undone or not forgiven. By forgiving you are adding another timeline and another time period to the event.

Remember, we were talking about the Records being frequencies. Any frequencies that lock parts of you "in place" or anchor you to a certain event or time period need to be reconciled. That way your "time stream" is clean—it becomes frequencies of beautiful, harmonious ribbons of colors as opposed to frequencies that would keep you locked in a place or time and cause you to reincarnate.

For example, you really wouldn't want a prior lifetime still affecting you today, keeping you from being free. This is what is interesting about reading your own Records or your own "Book"—you can see where you still have things to resolve. You can also see what you've *gained*—you can get a good measure of yourself.

Q. WHERE ARE THE RECORDS LOCATED?

A. Everywhere, throughout all existence. Even though the word *Akasha* implies a plane of Spirit, the truth is that the living field of information is recorded throughout all of existence, even in the cells of your body.

Q. ARE THERE DIFFERENT LOCATIONS FOR DIFFERENT UNIVERSES OR ARE THEY ALL IN THE SAME PLACE?

A. Again, it is about frequency. In one sense you could say that everything exists simultaneously, but you would not necessarily have *access* to every universe if you are not vibrationally compatible to it. Each person's Records are contained within the fields where they resonate and have had experiences.

Q. CAN ANYBODY GET INTO YOUR PERSONAL RECORDS?

A. Yes and no. If they can access your frequency, yes, but no, if their intention is not honorable or if there are lessons personal to you that need self-discovery. In those cases a blank wall of energy will appear, preventing them from reading.

The Records have their own safeguard against persons whose intentions are not honorable, in that such people's frequencies will not be high enough to access the Records. Anyone trying to read another's Records without their permission is not acting honorably. In principle, the Records are open books, but not in application. It's a perfect system.

Q. WHO ARE THE "LORDS" OF THE RECORDS?

A. They are beings whose job it is to "guard" the Records, meaning that they make sure each person's Records do not get mixed vibrationally with another's. They are *not* beings who demand any kind of permission. The Records have their own safeguards against those with impure intent.

Q. HOW DOES THAT MAKE SENSE IF WE'RE ALL THE SAME—IF AT A SPIRITUAL LEVEL WE'RE ALL ONE? WHY WOULD THERE BE BEINGS TO KEEP US SEPARATE IF WE ARE MEANT TO BE UNIFIED?

A. Each individual spirit is on its own journey to self-realization. You are misunderstanding "unified" or "one." Unity does not mean everyone dissolves into one thing. Unified means "in harmony with." It means that you understand that everything is in relationship with everything else—we all affect each other—it's a unified field in that way—but it doesn't mean that you don't have individuality. It is like the definition of love—love is the field of all that is—it doesn't mean it is one big identity in which you lose yours.

Q. IS THE NAME "LORDS" AN APPROPRIATE NAME FOR THEM?

A. Yes—the name "lord" in this case means "overseer" or guardian. It does not refer to any kind of adoration or hierarchy.

Q. DO YOU NEED TO ASK THESE LORDS FOR PERMISSION TO ACCESS THESE RECORDS?

A. No. It is their job to keep the Records in order. The permission to gain access is asked of the *person being read*, and it is they and their own higher aspects that agree to this.

Q. ARE THERE DIFFERENT LEVELS OF RECORDS, AND IF SO, WHERE ARE THEY AND WHAT DO THEY PERTAIN TO?

A. There are different levels of Records in that there are different universes and differing frequency ranges in those universes. The levels pertain to the experiences of those universes wherever they are, but information is accessible by anyone, anywhere.

Q. WHO ARE THE "MENTORS"? WHERE DO THEY COME FROM AND HOW ARE THEY ASSIGNED?

A. Mentors are spiritual beings from a collective sphere of Light who are specific to each person's soul journey. They are assigned at the birth of the spirit and remain with it throughout its journey within its galactic family. Some Mentors are attached to and follow spirit families rather than individual spirits. As the spirit ascends to higher universes, new mentors are assigned.

Q. WHAT CAN WE GAIN FROM ACCESSING OUR OWN AKASHIC RECORDS?

A. Accessing your Records will bring you a deep understanding of who you are and why you are here. You can understand health issues, lessons learned and yet to be learned, karmic imprints, relationships, and know your highest gifts and abilities.

You will also gain a greater appreciation for the value of choice and the effect choices have on your spiritual journey as well as their effect upon others and the whole. You will know *how much you matter* and how much a part of everything you are. You will know that you are loved and that life does indeed, make sense and have an order and purpose to it.

Who Are We

& Why are We Here?

Chapter 2

Who Are We and Why Are We Here?

In this discussion, the participants were looking for answers to their individual life purposes. It was the biggest group we had, revealing the confusion and sense of feeling "lost" that people are experiencing in today's world. Source, however, had a very different answer to the question, "Who are we and why are we here?" than we expected. The information takes us back to a much bigger perspective of ourselves and to an ancient history that we have forgotten.

Q. WHO ARE WE AND WHY ARE WE HERE?

A. Many of us have been coming here to Earth from the beginning, before the Earth was green and had water. It was a sphere of white/yellow swirling energy. We were in our original spirit forms. We were among "the first swirlings," as we were swirling around this sphere.

We have been watching and developing this planet for many millions of years. It is an exciting event in the cosmos when new "spheres" come into being. Source itself is delighted with new formations as they appear and sends out its creations to explore the new spheres as they appear and bring back the joy and delight to Source.

Our particular sphere, which we call Earth, went from a white light sphere to an emerald green sphere as it slowed in its motion. When spheres first come off of Source, they are spinning at a particular rate. Over billions of years the rate of spin begins to slow and as it does, the spheres take on particular color bands. The color band representing the Earth is emerald green.

When we as spirit beings choose to come close to a new planet, we begin to take on the frequency bands of that sphere. This is why many of us resonate with the emerald green color, why many of the healing systems use emerald green light, why we see the plant kingdom as emerald green, *etc.*

The "density" of the sphere as it coalesces determines the color band or frequency at which it resonates. For example, if a sphere becomes denser, it would take on a denser color band such as red or orange. If the sphere was less dense, it would take on a less dense color band such as blue or violet, *etc.*

Q. WHY DO BEINGS COME HERE?

A. They come for *joy*. They come to celebrate Source! "Heaven" is thrilled when new creations come into being! Beings come to celebrate the new creation. This is the purpose for *anything* that is created from Source. When these beings (we) first came, they were delighted to be able to bring forth life here. Source is interested in developing what we call "paradises," and this is what this planet was originally. It is *we* who were among the beings of the first swirlings.

Q. WHY ARE HUMANS AT THE "TOP OF THE CHAIN"?

A. Source finds this question amusing because we have digressed so far from what we were originally. The way we are now is not the way we were originally. There was a "mishap" or a "fall" that occurred on the original Paradise Earth which caused a dimensional split of the Earth. When this occurred, many of the original beings were fragmented *spiritually* - some retained their original spirit self intact, others were split in their spirit bodies by the dimensional split that occurred during the fall. After the fall, the original beings who were still intact kept trying to recreate the life forms on fallen Earth to be as close as possible to their original perfect spiritual templates.

Our original beings were not dense like we are now. When the fall occurred, two-thirds of the planet and its species fell into a denser form. The original beings who remained intact tried to maintain as much of the original connection to Source as they could. Even from that change, which was a "step-down" from our original spirit selves, we today are even more downstepped than that. The various species of humans, animals, birds, plant life and insects, as you know them now, are the result of the fall, in that they are much denser in form than they were in the beginning. The original species mentioned above as well as dolphins, whales, and trees, were more like "wave forms." The "fall" was a sudden event that occurred which caused a division similar to an abyss, or a chasm between Paradise Earth and the now fallen piece of Earth. The original beings that came to Earth did not want to lose the part of Earth that fell and its species, so they also went to the fallen Earth to continue to develop life there. By doing so, they too had to "fall" to the now-denser planet to match its frequency in order to continue to evolve life there. Densification continued as a process on fallen Earth, as other species from other lower dimensional spaces came to fallen Earth wanting to live there also. This caused conflicts and wars between the original beings who were on a repair mission and lesser beings from outside who were now all vying for control over fallen Earth. After eons of genetically experimenting with the life forms on fallen Earth, the current species-human, plant and animal species residing on fallen Earth is the result of these genetic modifications. It is clear this is no t what we were in the beginning—we were not this dense.

The impact of the dimensional split, or fall, of Paradise Earth resulted in the spiritual fracture of many of its inhabitants. This means that their once perfect spiritual nature fell to an unnatural vibration, causing a lower or "split" being. Many of the problems we encounter today are because many of us retain *two memories* in our *spirits*—one of our paradise self and the other of our fallen self. Some would call this our *split mind,* but it is actually at the level of our spirit bodies where the distortion has had its effect. We believe we are both—perfect and fallen, and have been desperately trying to reconcile both realities within us, causing great conflict within us. We cannot reconcile these two parts because they are incompatible with each other. To repair this, we must be willing to choose to be only our original Paradise self once again. Because we hold the memory of it spiritually, we can bring it back into being by choosing *only it.* We cannot serve two masters. You can see that this split into two separate identities is the cause of the identity crisis we have on this planet. It is why we are vulnerable to authority figures who want to tell us who we are and how we are to be.

This is the Big Picture answer to why we are not at the top of the chain!

Q. WHAT HAPPENED TO CAUSE THE FALL?

A. First, let's go back and say that Source does not deliberately create the spheres that come off of It. They are the result of what's going on in the cosmos—in other words they are a result of vibrations and chemical reactions that are occurring. The fall occurred when a powerful vibration or wave hit Earth and split it. The impact was so immense that it actually caused a "dimensional split," causing everything here to suddenly become fragmented. *No beings caused this,* but some beings from other dimensions definitely took advantage of this dimensional split. We are talking only of the "fall" for "Earth" and not of other types of "falls" in the cosmos.

Q. IS IT THE CASE THAT DENSER BEINGS CAME TO EARTH AND COLONIZED IT?

A. Not right away. Initially, the wave strike caused a division that cracked the Earth and split it off into two pieces, leaving a huge gap in between, similar to a chasm in outer space.

Q. WAS THIS SPLIT INTO TWO EQUAL PIECES? ARE WE BACK TOGETHER NOW?

A. It was not in equal pieces, and no, we are not back together with the "original" piece. Two-thirds fell into greater density and only one-third remained in its original Paradise frequency. We are now on the fallen piece in order to raise it up to its original Paradise frequency. Remember we were the original beings who took this planet on as our "baby." We had and still *do* have an investment in Earth's growth and evolution. It is why we have incarnated here in these dense bodies—we still want to raise this planet to its original Paradise frequency.

After the fall with the densification that ensued, we also took on these bodies in this densification. We have all been working for eons to get this fallen piece reconnected. It cannot reconnect however, as long as its frequency is low.

We have not come here every lifetime, however, but most of us would have continued to come in every major transition cycle when the opportunities to reconnect or "ascend" to Paradise Earth is greater. We choose to come in as a collective for this repair mission.

Denser beings from other dimensions came here because the Earth's fall into densification attracted them as they were of like kind *vibrationally*. They resonated with this fallen piece and have lived here for many eons. They do not welcome us coming in here to raise this piece back up to its Paradise aspect because they have considered fallen Earth their home for many eons and cycles.

When we succeed, they will no longer be compatible with this piece unless their personal frequencies change and rise also. They do not want us to succeed, and they will try anything to keep us from succeeding. This is why the battles between light and dark, or between "less dense beings" and "denser beings" ensued and continues to this day. Many of *us* have actually become "caught" in the densification ourselves. We have developed person- alities or egos that resonate with the densification, resulting in us *losing our memory* of who we are.

This is part of the reason you are all here tonight—to remember who you are and why you are here. Think of yourselves in a huge way and of the billions of years that have gone by since the first swirling. Many of you have lived lifetimes here between cycles that were very much "personality lives" resulting in the forgetting of who you were originally.

Because we have done this, we have accumulated our own personal karma, which now has to be balanced out within this creation because this is where we made it. But now we are in a cosmic cycle that is allowing for accelerated karmic resolution and memory awakening. Forgiveness is the way to accomplish this.

We are seeing many people now wanting to remember or knowing it is time to remember. Let's get on with it. You are all part of the original beings—it is why you are here. You knew this planet when it was first a sphere of Light.

Because so many of us have fallen into density, we all say we just want out. We say we know this isn't "Home"—that we don't belong here—it must be a mistake that we are here, *etc.* but we actually *do* belong here—Earth is our baby that we are trying to raise up.

Q. DID WE DECIDE TO COME BACK HERE NOW BECAUSE WE ARE IN A CYCLE?

A. Yes. It is the biggest purpose we came back for, and we decided it as a collective. It isn't just about cleaning up your personal karma. The picture is much bigger. There are large groups of us here—some are angelic humans—others have come from other spheres and were also part of the original beings who seeded Earth in the beginning. We all need to rethink the part of us that says we just want to get out of here—it isn't what we decided. We want out because we don't like the density here—but we came here as a rescue mission to raise this piece of Earth to its ascended place.

Q. WHAT IS THE BALANCE OF PLAY AT THIS POINT? ARE WE WINNING OR LOSING?

A. Let's talk about the "other piece" of Earth first—the part that *didn't* fall—the "ascended" piece that is still a Paradise. That piece is *not* Parallel Earth—it is Ascension Earth. That piece is very much on line with Source's original intention and divine blueprint. However, that ascended piece has not evolved as far as it could have gone because it is still corded to this fallen piece we are on. We humans have split spirits because we are still corded to both pieces.

Q. WERE ANY OF US EVER ON THAT OTHER PIECE SINCE IT SPLIT (THE PARADISE PIECE)?

A. Absolutely. It is why we all have a memory of Paradise.

Q. IS THAT WHAT "HEAVEN" IS?

A. First, let's go into the split mind a bit more. It is why we all have this battle within. We are carrying the imprints of both events inside our biology! We can change our biology by changing our spiritual focus. By switching your perception or focus of attention, you can switch which *reality* you are in. You can do this because both realities are *within* your spirit body.

Q. SO, WHAT IS "HEAVEN"?

A. Heaven is *all* of the creations that have come off of Source. "Source" itself would be considered Heaven with all the worlds we are speaking about. If a person who is on the fallen piece of Earth were to die and they only went to the Paradise piece of Earth, they would think they were in Heaven, compared to this fallen piece.

Q. IS THE FALL AND PARADISE WHERE THE ADAM AND EVE STORY CAME FROM?

A. Yes. But let's explain. Before the fall, procreation was done by *thought*. There was no need for reproduction as we know it now. All beings emerged as spheres by thought intention. Remember that the original species could ascend and move freely throughout creation. The original species was also androgynous—both male and female. They could easily ascend, which meant the ability to move freely in and out of many dimensional spaces and easily "procreate" by thought intention or agreement.

There was no split into male and female. All aspects were contained within each being. When things fell and the split occurred, it caused fragmentation within the beings that fell with the falling piece of Earth. Because of this, experimentation with denser forms ensued to try to create a type of denser being that could reconnect to Source from this now fallen piece.

Because of the fragmentation, the ability to create by thought was not as easy as before. The ability to create new beings by thought was lost, and the androgynous nature was now split into pieces. Adam and Eve were the first split-*matter* beings. They became male and female with the creation of reproductive organs. The idea that Adam and Eve disobeyed God refers to the fact that this down-stepping into fragmented matter beings was not Source's original intention.

Source's creations are whole. However, Adam and Eve did not cause the fall—they were an *effect* of it.

Q. IS THIS THE EVENT WHEN THE TWIN FLAMES SPLIT?

A. No. The twin flame splitting was a decision on higher levels beyond our 3-D Earth. Twins still each held their androgyny or their original blueprint.

Splitting of this type is similar to how a cell divides and reproduces or how spheres emerge out of Source. In terms of "time," twin splitting happened many millions of eons ago and did not occur on Earth.

Q. Where does Darwin's Theory of Evolution come in?

A. Darwin's theory is more about the experimentation with different prototypes after the fall. He was intuiting some type of *evolution* by seeing various types of species that resembled each other in certain ways. It was not really evolution as Darwin perceived it to be—rather it was genetic experimentation on a grand scale.

Q. Are we all slowly evolving back to the original Earth or Paradise?

A. In truth, we still hold the memory and biology of the original Paradise sphere. Remember I said we are still corded to the original Paradise piece. There is nowhere to *evolve* back *to*, as Paradise Earth is still *within* our spirit bodies. But it has everything to do with which piece we identify ourselves with. This decision determines which reality you are a part of and resonate with. Both spheres are in our spirits—fallen Earth and Ascension Earth.

Where we get stuck is when we think we are *only* these matter beings or *fallen* identities. As long as we identify ourselves with dense-matter biology—past life identities included—we forget that our *Paradise self* is also *within* us. When we talk about "resurrecting" this fallen Earth to Paradise Earth, we understand that we first have to correct the "split" that has occurred in our spirits and filters down to our minds, which leaves us with a memory of two Earths. This "spirit split" is the reason why we perceive Light *and* dark—the memory of both is in our spirits.

The problem is we cannot serve two masters—but *one* has to be chosen to resurrect this fallen piece. Choose light *or* dark, love *or* fear—but not both together as it has been.

Q. IS THE REINTEGRATION WITHIN US OF THESE PARTS WHAT SPIRITUAL WORK IS ABOUT?

A. It is not about integrating the split parts—rather it is about choosing that you are the original, or Paradise, spirit that is the only "real" you. Now that you know that you are still your Paradise self, you need to change your biology back to your original self by *choosing only it.*

The biology takes direction from the spirit's belief about who and what it is. This signal tells the biology what to do. If we give it the signal that we are a dense-matter being subject to disease, death and imperfection, this is what our cells will produce. If on the other hand we give the biology the signal that we are a perfect, androgynous Paradise self, this is what our cells will produce.

The choice is ours, and it is something we choose every moment. In actuality, we are either the fallen beings or our original beings—which will we choose to identify with?

Our split spirit allows us to believe in two realities and two selves, but never at the same time. We have to choose Paradise in order to make it *all* Paradise. It must be realized that *we* are the fallen beings and the fallen Earth as long as we identify with that version of ourselves.

Consider why history repeats itself—it is because we are not identifying with our Paradise selves, who are very real biological realities within us. To most of us, Paradise is something that existed a very long time ago, certainly not *now*. It is in the far-distant memories of our minds. However, it is also a *now* reality in our bodies and minds. The *c(h)ords* are still there, waiting for us to activate them within us with our attention. It is *we* who decide.

Once the fall happened, it naturally attracted species and beings of like vibration from around the cosmos. The more who came here, the more they interfered with those of us who were trying to fix the split. We were trying to raise the frequency of the fallen piece to *bridge it back* to the original piece. We have been continually interfered with energetically, religiously and biologically, and we have not yet made the progress back to the original piece.

Q. WHERE DID THE "OTHERS" WHO CAME TO EARTH AFTER THE FALL COME FROM?

A. They came from many places in the cosmos. Remember that when things offshoot from Source they eventually coalesce at many varying vibrations and frequencies. The piece of Earth that fell was now at a different rate of vibration, attracting species of like kind. Their goal now is keeping the denser piece of Earth dense, and this is the fight we are in. The original beings are trying to bring Earth back together and the denser beings want to keep the two pieces separate. Again, many of us have fallen into this density and have forgotten "who we are and why we are here."

Q. ARE THE BEINGS IN THE DENSER FORM IN HUMAN FORM AS WELL?

A. Oh, absolutely. In fact, they would love to keep the body as dense and divided as they can to favor the animalistic side of things. They are fondly into bodily pleasures, materialism and control.

Q. DO THEY KNOW WHAT THEY ARE DOING?

A. Some do consciously; most do not know. The conscious ones are actively keeping this planet dense, and the others are simply "dense humans" — asleep in their consciousness with little or no memory of Paradise.

Q. THEN THERE IS NO EVIL, JUST DIFFERENT DENSITIES OF FORM WITH THEIR OWN PURPOSES?

A. It would be nice to say it that way, but if you continue to go down the scale of density, you will get to densities that many would consider evil. Source would not label them evil, however, but they are no longer modeling the original androgynous intention of Source. In English, "evil" is the word "live" spelled backwards, indicating the degree of reversal away from the original life intention. Source has said the motivation for those that attempt to reverse the life principle is against Source's intention, which is Love. Love is harmless intention and expression.

Q. IS IT IMPORTANT NOW TO BRING THE POLARIZATION BACK INTO ALIGNMENT?

A. The thing about this fallen piece is that it isn't balanced with the Paradise piece. They are not equally polarized. You can see evidence of this in the one-third light and two-thirds dark. It seems to us who are here on this fallen piece that it takes a lot more effort to stay positive than it does to be negative. Each piece functions at a very different rate of vibration. In order for them to be reconciled, you have to *raise* the fallen piece up to the *frequency* of the Paradise piece and this has to be done *within* each one of us in order for it to manifest in the "outer."

Dark and light are not equal. Every thought we think, every action we take, every perception we have, either reinforces the fallen piece or contributes to Paradise Earth. You have to resolve this within your own biology. Dark and light do not come together, because they can't. Within our own biology, you have to rise *up* to the Paradise self.

Q. WHAT ARE WE SUPPOSED TO DO WITH OUR FALLEN SELF OR SHADOW—INTEGRATE IT OR TRANSFORM IT?

A. Transform it. Your shadow is a collection of beliefs and perceptions that you are choosing to believe in. When you choose your original self, the shadow, or fallen, self is no longer active.

Q. IT'S NOT PART OF YOUR ORIGINAL BEING THEN?

A. No. It is a result of the splitting of the spirit into two *experiences*. One experience is Paradise; the other experience is of falling out or away from Paradise Earth. Both experiences are memories in our spirits. We originally came to this fallen piece to create the bridge that would unite both pieces back together, but in the process of being in this densification, many of us have forgotten who we are and why we came here.

Q. BY COMING BACK HERE AND TAKING THIS PIECE ON, AS "OUR BABY," AS YOU PUT IT, ARE WE NOT ALSO CHOOSING OUR SHADOW, IN A SENSE, BECAUSE IT'S PART OF THE PARCEL?

A. No, you are not *choosing* your shadow; it is part of the *consequence* of taking on this density. You can't transform the shadow by believing in it. You have to choose to believe in your original self *only* in order to have it come alive or active within you. What you are choosing to believe is what you are telling your biology to *be*. This is a quantum truth.

Q. SO IT'S REALLY WHAT ALL THE GREAT SPIRITUAL WRITERS ARE SAYING—TO CHOOSE IN EVERY MOMENT?

A. Perfection over imperfection, life over death, joy over suffering, health over disease, abundance over poverty, love over hate, harmlessness over harm. I want to be clear that Paradise is in your *cells*. Your cells take instruction from *you*. You give the signal. *You decide!*

Q. WHO'S DOING THE CHOOSING?

A. You as your Spirit self is doing the choosing. If you become so dense that you no longer remember Paradise, then you won't choose it—you won't have the *awareness* to choose. Your Spirit is asleep to you, and you won't hear its voice.

The advantage of the cosmic cycle we are now in is that the higher frequencies of Light are coming in, which allows for the *triggering* or *activation* of memory or truth to occur within the biology for everyone. This gives everyone an opportunity to choose and change.

Q. WHY WEREN'T WE AWAKENED EARLIER?

A. The "you" that is here knows what you are doing on an *inner* level. You do have to wait for cosmic cycles for *accelerated opportunities* to occur. Many lifetimes have been spent in lower vibrations and dogmas. Very few of us know how to be our own authority. To show this, look how easily fear can come up for us. For example, look at how fearful people are who are waking up and who have also been brought up in religious families—they are terrified to go against the grain and be true to themselves. And this is just one tiny example.

Q. ARE THE FEARS WE ALL HAVE—FINANCES, DEATH, RELATIONSHIPS, GOVERNMENT, *ETC.*—WHAT'S KEEPING US ALL IN THE LOWER FREQUENCIES?

A. Yes, absolutely.

Q. IF WE COULD GET TO THE PLACE WHERE WE ARE NOT IN FEAR ANYMORE, WHERE WE CHOOSE THE PARADISE REALITY, WOULD THE FEAR THEN DISSOLVE AWAY?

A. Yes, because in the Paradise reality there is no fear, only direct communication with Source and "All That Is."

Q. ARE THE COSMIC CYCLES WHY WE HAVEN'T BEEN ABLE TO WAKE UP, BECAUSE OF THE PRECESSION OF THE EQUINOXES—THE GREAT COSMIC WHEEL? DO WE HAVE TO WAIT FOR THAT?

A. No, the waking up could have happened earlier if, in the interplay of light vs. dark, different choices had been made—if the species had made different choices the quantum balance would/could still have tipped the scales toward Paradise Earth, our Paradise selves and the Light. What cosmic cycles provide are *accelerated opportunities* and *cellular activations of memory.*

Q. DO THE DARK FORCES KEEP US ASLEEP BY DULLING OUR MINDS SO WE CAN'T CHOOSE?

A. Yes. It is true that the dark forces use anything they can to keep us asleep, but it is we who choose to follow them or not.

In summary, this inquiry into "Who Are We and Why Are We Here?" revealed to us that *we* are the original etheric Light Beings who came first to this new swirling light planet to seed life here.

Through an event in the cosmos, the Earth split into two pieces—one larger piece "fell" to a denser vibration, and the other piece—the smaller piece—remained in its original Paradise vibration.

Many of us keep returning to this fallen or denser piece to try to "save it," to bring it back up to its original Paradise piece, but as a result of coming here, many of us fell into the denser vibration and forgot who we were or why we came. We got caught in a cycle of light and dark, and the laws of cause and effect came into being. Being subject to these laws, we were now in the cycle of "karma" and subject to reincarnation in order to balance out this karma.

It is important to realize that cause and effect and karma did not exist before the fall. They are the result of our split minds, which were a consequence of the Earth fall.

The present cosmic cycle we are in offers us an influx of great Light in which to wake up to the memory of who we are and choose our Paradise selves once again. In doing so, we not only resurrect ourselves, but we also resurrect the fallen/dense Earth and all species that inhabit it.

"Paradises" are what Source Creator desires for all its creations.

This is "Who You Are and Why You are Here."

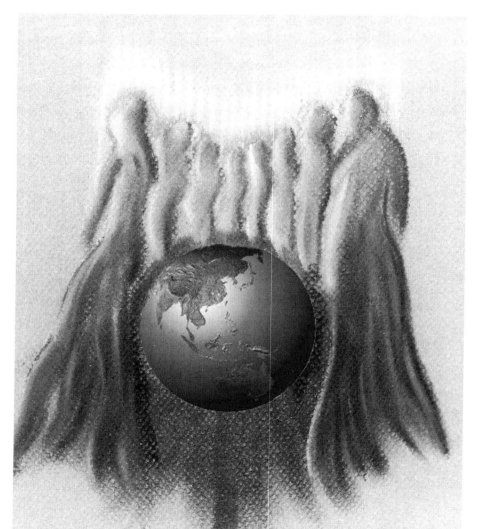

Our Organic
True Selves

Chapter 3

Our Organic True Selves

As we begin this session, there is a group of very large, beautiful Light Beings coming towards us. They actually look like a huge star fleet, but I don't see a ship. There are no ships, just these Beings coming towards us. Oh! They are us—they are the *real* us.

Briefly, let me mention that a *sovereign being* does not need a spaceship, *ever*. Source is being really clear about that. The necessity for ships has come from forgetting the ability to be the organic true self as God created us. God Source has created us so huge, you can't even imagine it. So powerful. So free. So able and capable.

Q. ARE THESE BEINGS WHO ARE COMING TOWARDS US LIKE ANGELS?

A. No, they do not have wings. They are huge, white, flowing, ethereal Light Beings. There are no ships involved. They are vertical, very tall beings. They are coming towards us precisely because of our topic tonight.

They are being very specific about language because of the vibration of words. To call our true selves that are coming toward us "angels" is not a strong enough word, nor is it accurate for what I am being shown. The force of these Beings is very great. They are tall and huge; they are all together, and the collective of them is coming towards us. What we would call an "angel" is actually a very different frequency band and a very different aspect of us. Our true selves that are coming toward us are much bigger than angelic beings. They also do not want to be called extraterrestrials (ETs).

They are our "true selves as Source/God created us," and they wouldn't want to be named anything else. They are telling us that the term "ET" is a down-step. They would not want to be labeled anything like that. They are our magnificent pure selves off of Source! That's a word they say we can use—"magnificent"! They are coming to merge with us now to facilitate our "resurrection."

As they come towards us and merge with us, our biology will become increasingly purified. Our biology will become "organic" once again as it was when we were originally created by Source. That's why it is called the "resurrection."

"Resurrection" means that your body, your biology, and your energy fields are put back to the way they were originally. It is so complete; I can even feel our bones changing. We are not talking here about raising someone who has already died. We are talking about the living.

Just to be clear, they are saying "resurrection" really does mean physical resurrection of the *already living*. It affects the physical biology. The kind of resurrection I am seeing has not occurred in a very long time. We have gone through cycles of light ages and dark ages, but we have now come to a time where the potential for biological resurrection is being divinely orchestrated.

Q. WHAT IS ASCENSION?

A. "Ascension" is when you actually *are* your true self and you are a free being once again. That is what is called your ascension. Your physical body is transmuted into a light vehicle—every part of the physical biology changes and is now able to be its true self. And when it is its true self, you are an ascended being, which means you are *free*.

Source says: "Ascension is when you merge with *me*."

Q. I WANT TO KNOW MORE ABOUT "OUR TRUE SELVES THAT ARE COMING TOWARDS US." I'M VERY CURIOUS—I FEEL THEIR FREQUENCY HERE TONIGHT, IN THIS ROOM, AND I WANT TO KNOW IF IT WILL CONTINUE AFTER WE LEAVE HERE TONIGHT?

A. Yes, this contact will continue after tonight, if that is your desire. Your true organic selves are the "you" that has come direct from Source and has never left Source. They are also "your future selves" talked about previously. If you take yourself back far enough, back through your many lifetimes on Earth and on other planets, you will eventually return to the "you" that first came off of Source.

This is your *true organic self* (and they're very clear about the phrase) that has come to merge with you. It's more of an integration with you than it is a division between a higher being and yourself. The contact you feel from them tonight on your right shoulder was made to show you that they're real and that it's possible for the merging to happen.

This merger with you is called a "resurrection" because it will raise your biology into a much higher frequency. Your true self is the self that has never been distorted, never been attacked, never been down-stepped. Consider your true self to be the self that God Source has held in its mind for you. The crystals in your body will activate, so it's a perfect time for you to be aware of your own internal crystal network that can be regenerated.

The crystals in every cell will begin spinning faster. It is wise, if you want to have this merger happen, to make sure you're letting yourself shift over to more foods that are compatible with that. You will naturally desire more water and fresh juices. You may find that you suddenly desire different foods, or you will no longer be able to tolerate foods you have been eating in the past.

Your own abilities of telepathic communication will increase. You will receive more inspiration and higher thoughts. You will feel a strength and peace in you that you did not have before. You will have greater immunity to illnesses. Being aware of the "one movement" of all life will also increase.

Your true selves are you; they are not separate beings. Their name is "your true organic selves"—the *you* that is already masterful and one with Source.

One of the things that's important to know with this merging is that this is you *becoming* and *returning* to your true self, physically and in every other way. That's the real meaning of "resurrection."

Resurrection is not about dying first and being raised from the dead. Resurrection is for the living. To correct this old idea of resurrection—it's not about coming back for an already dead body. A dead body cannot be resurrected. Only a living body can be resurrected.

Q. HAVE OUR TRUE ORGANIC SELVES BEEN WITHIN OUR REALM OF MERGER ALL ALONG, OR IS MY ORGANIC SELF NOW MAKING THE CHOICE TO MERGE WITH ME?

A. No, they haven't been in your realm all along. You've had a higher self that's been your go-between, and it's been a bridge for you.

They have not had the opportunity before now to come in and merge with us. There's an amount of time that's been allotted for every soul to go through lifetimes and to go through karmic learning to advance to a certain level of awareness on its own.

We've been in time, while our true selves are beyond time—they have nothing to do with time. Time itself is on its way out, as we know it. We have been under the arc of time, like a canopy, for eons.

Now we're at a point where time itself is due to collapse, or "speed up." Our true organic selves have not had permission to come and merge with us, because a certain amount of time was given souls to learn and experience at a certain rate of vibration.

You may feel fear at times, or you might wonder what's happening to you, or you might feel disoriented. This is part of the small self being rearranged cellularly. And please use those words "true organic self" or "organic true self." That word, "organic" is very important.

As your true self merges with you, time is going to collapse for you personally. Until then, you are part of this whole collective process of the collapse of time, of bringing back the truth on all the different levels as it manifests itself, until you're done. You're going to know when you're done.

No space ship is coming to get you—those are false teachings. No true being needs a ship, ever. Please understand the degree of manipulation of those teachings that tell you that some ship is going to come and take you Home. "Home" is you merging with your true self.

While we're still under the veils of time, this shifting is a process. Right now we're still held in place by the laws of gravity. The law of gravity is the law of karma. Gravity and the law of karma are the same thing.

Q. SO WHEN YOU'RE OFF THE KARMIC WHEEL, THERE WILL BE NO MORE GRAVITY?

A. Yes, that's right. Density is the collective karma of everybody. That's what keeps us heavy.

When the wheel of karma is over, there's no more gravity. Now you know why forgiveness is so important—why releasing the victim/victimizer belief has to happen.

If you're going to believe in the victim/victimizer process, you're going to stay in gravity. The reason the physical body is so dense is because it's made up of grievances and false perceptions.

Q. IS OUR PLANET GOING INTO ANOTHER DIMENSION, OR ARE ALL OF US ASCENDING INTO ANOTHER DIMENSION?

A. The Earth was chuckling when I ran that question through. First of all, in answer to your question, we are in a *collective* movement—it's not just Earth vs. us, it's a collective movement.

The Earth would say we're moving into a different *frequency* and a *different way of life*. We are ascending to finer energies or higher frequencies, but in terms of her actually moving into another dimensional space, she's saying it's not that way.

It's more of a rise in frequency and a change for all the biological life forms on the planet to move into a different biology. So will you actually go to a new place? Earth chuckles when you ask that question, and she says, "Not really, it's not quite like that. It's more of an evolving shift in biology."

Q. IS THIS AN OPPORTUNITY FOR HUMAN BEINGS TO SHIFT WITH THE EARTH? IS IT OUR CONSCIOUSNESS THAT SHIFTS, OR OUR BIOLOGY?

A. Consciousness is perception, and it is also frequency. When you shift a perception, you also shift in frequency. We're hoping that the consciousness of the people will shift into new, healthier perceptions.

When the collective consciousness changes, your biology will begin to change also. If you want to keep moving through this, you need water; you need to be aware of your thoughts, and you need to watch your choices. What choices are you making?

The Earth is not taking off without us—we all move together. Earth is being really clear though, that the life forms on the planet will be changing, and that's why you'll see some species die off. If the species is making a decision not to mutate their biology, then we'll see it leave. As well as the new children coming in, you'll see new plants and new animals emerge. The Earth is telling me that that's the movement at the biological level.

So, it's not only what you're aware of in your perception—it's also happening to your biology. The influx of Light coming in is promoting not only this shift in consciousness, but this biological shift as well.

Q. HOW CAN WE BE MORE ASCENSION READY?

A. If we could focus only on one thing, it would be to focus only on Love; how to be more loving, how to love ourselves. Source is reminding us that It is made of Love, life is made of Love, and we're made of Love. Even though that may seem ethereal, it really isn't, because Love is an abiding principle or law that works throughout the Universe, which says that to give is to receive. Everyone gives and receives equally all the time.

Ascension readiness is a purification process of loving—to love yourself and others and to become Love. Look into areas of your life where love may not be maximal. For example, we recently found out in the Akashic Records that our individual spirits—not our souls—can experience trauma.

The spirit self is the you that is the thinker, the decider and the experiencer. How your spirit experiences life will determine how it forms a concept of itself. Your spirit self may have many areas where you still feel injured or are carrying trauma or things unhealed or unforgiven. Even a simple rejection could still be held in your spirit. Because of these things, it can be really difficult to love yourself fully or to love others. There would be blockages where Love could not get through. To the degree that we are hurting or not releasing trauma, our love is limited in our ability to give love to others and to ourselves. If you have been a meditator for many years and have experienced the higher levels, you know that the higher you go, the more loving it gets. You cannot carry any type of negativity into the higher frequencies of Love.

So to be ascension ready, see how well you love yourself, see anything unhealed or unforgiven, and let go or release anything that is holding you back from loving in the best way you possibly can.

Q. FROM WHOM DO WE SEEK HELP TO RELEASE TRAUMA AND INJURY FROM OUR SPIRITS?

A. I hear Source saying, "Why don't you just go directly to Me, that God Source that lives within you?" Source means that literally, because who better than the Source of all life to go to? Who else would have the answer to everything you could possibly want to know or need help with? It's the simplest and easiest answer. Source is reminding us that it is made of Love itself. Our problems on this dimension are that we really don't understand what that love of Source really means and how it would feel and express itself to us in our everyday life. How would it apply to a human walking around in a physical body here on Earth? The reason that Source wants us to go directly to It within us, is because we need to be shown what that love is. The only way we're going to be able to really understand it, is for Source to show it to us directly.

Q. HOW CAN WE SEE OR HEAR THE ANSWERS OR MESSAGES FROM SOURCE IF WE CAN'T MEDITATE OR STILL OUR MINDS TO BE ABLE TO HEAR SOURCE SPEAKING TO US?

A. Source gave me the answer before you finished the question! Do you really think the only way Source can communicate with us is through meditation? Source will answer each person in the way they can recognize. Source will pick the form or the way of communicating that can be received and understood by the individual asking for it. For one person it could be through meditation, for another it could be through a new job or relationship or a feather on the ground or a bird flying in the sky at just the right moment. The possibilities are endless!

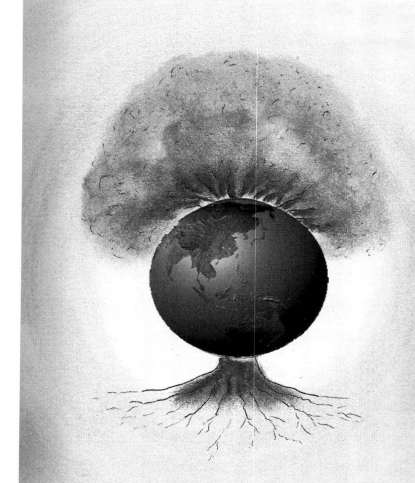

Health

Chapter 4

Health

When I said the opening prayer, the room filled with beautiful blue light. The feeling I had about this blue light is that every one of you here is a representative of truth. Each one is a pillar of truth to the world, so I want to acknowledge your spirit presences for being here.

This is really about a time of mastery for all of us. Learning about our bodies and our own energetic system is a smart and necessary thing to do, so that your dependence on other people, or drug companies, to fix you becomes less and less. There is no excuse for us not to be learning about ourselves and how we personally may be contributing to the issues we are experiencing in our lives.

Increasing your own intuitive abilities and asking your own body why it is out of balance is a good practice. When you are unhappy or unclear about things just ask, "What is going on with me?"

This is paramount in this time of change because it is going to determine who can move through these changes and come out ahead of the game, as opposed to those who it's going to affect in a detrimental way. This whole process we're in lessens our dependence on outside authorities upon whom we've been so dependent upon until now.

Q. What can Source share with us that we could do to improve our health and help the Earth at this time?

A. Every one of us is a *starburst* that emanates out like a huge burst of Light from the area of our sternum. Our ability to cast Light everywhere is *huge*, but we let our intellect get in the way. Source is advising us to stop the thinking—stop the brain fog. It is interfering with our ability to be aware of the Light that we *are* and can give. We're already beings of Light and Sound, and we block the flow of this Light by focusing on our small and petty concerns. We make everything too complicated.

Source put Itself *in* you. "I have put My Self in you, so stop making a mess of it. Your brain wiring looks like a tangled ball of yarn. Your ability to give and share with each other is huge. Stop holding onto things—instead, *give* to each other."

There is no reason for anyone to be comfortless—we all have plenty of resources to give and share. I see hands extended outward to others. Source tells us to:

- Stop hoarding
- Walk more
- Take time to commune with ourselves *and* our God Source within us.
- Meditate daily on our true nature in silent prayer.

Get away from being so worried about self-preservation. We're all connected, and we're all safe, so what are we all so worried about? We create much of our own chaos and illness through our own worries, fear thoughts and guilt perceptions. More love is the answer, for yourself and for others.

Our ability to heal is much greater than we imagine. To give to another is to give to yourself. You can offer light; you can offer love and compassion. It's up to the other person if they'll receive it. When a person is in distress, they're not in their will.

You can offer a loving thought; you can bless them with your mind; and you can reinforce the God within them with your thoughts. You don't have to figure anything out, because it's all perfectly done.

Our biggest issue is we're all caught up in our individual selves. Source is saying help, give, and share. Make it a community happening. Get to know your neighbors—find out who needs help. There's no excuse for not helping; there's plenty to share, even in a small area. It's not about striving, it's about *communing.*

Q. IS HAIR DYE HARMFUL TO ONE'S HEALTH?

A. Topically it only reaches the surface layers of the scalp, and its effects are temporary, since it is washed off readily. Inhalation of the chemicals as it is being applied is a different story, however. Inhalation puts a toxic load inside the body that is hard to get rid of, like heavy metals. People who work with these chemicals frequently are at greater health risk. These chemicals weaken the thyroid gland.

Q. WHY CAN'T WE BRING SOMEONE BACK FROM THE DEAD?

A. Because it's each individual's choice to die. When the belief in death is replaced with the possibility of living indefinitely, you will see this change.

Q. WHEN GRAINS ARE SO IMPORTANT TO THE OVERALL DIET, WHY ARE WE SEEING SO MANY PEOPLE WHO CANNOT TOLERATE GLUTEN THESE DAYS?

A. It is due to a gradual weakening of the immune systems of people in general due to increasing environmental pollutants and processed foods. Increased sensitivity to pesticides and fungicides on crops also contributes to this weakening as does widespread fungi and bacteria. When this occurs, the digestive and eliminative processes in the body are compromised. Some individuals are born with highly sensitive systems already and need organic, unprocessed foods right from the start.

Q. IS IT THE NATURAL ORDER OF THINGS THAT PEOPLE SHOULD EAT MEAT, OR SHOULD WE BECOME VEGETARIANS?

A. This is more about the evolution of consciousness and a species rather than a *natural order*. When we look at the human race and nature as it is, the consuming of other life forms throughout nature, we assume this is *natural order*. In actuality, this only reflects the consciousness of a planet and its inhabitants. This is not the way it is on other planetary systems, although some are still this way.

As many of you may have noticed, in the past few years there has been increasing evidence in the animal kingdom of species that would be natural enemies nursing one another's young, or playing and cuddling with one another rather than killing for food. More humans are moving towards less dense foods, more organic foods. Some people have *graduated* to living on light. As consciousness matures, you will see what we consider the *natural order* move towards a more light-based form of being fed. This will take a long time, but it is part of *natural* consciousness expansion as planets and species evolve more towards being *strictly* love based.

In this process—and it is a *process*—people will naturally desire less dense foods and move towards *lighter* foods that are easier to digest. This is not something to be forced, but it is a natural, easy progression for an individual. As consciousness changes, and the species becomes more love based, the idea of killing for food will seem revolting. We will move toward the sacredness of all life. At this point, you will be looking at *biologies changing* to live more on light. This will also include the animal species. Consciousness plays a major role in determining the types of life forms that appear on a planet. If the planet itself were to shift to a higher frequency, it would naturally change all the biologies of all the species on the planet, or they would die out.

Q. IS MEAT INTRINSICALLY BAD, OR IS IT HOW IT IS RAISED AND WHAT IT CONTAINS?

A. Meat is not bad. Many biologies are designed to need it in relation to their consciousness, as they are at the moment. Others thrive on a vegetarian diet, as they are so inclined. As people's frequencies rise, they will desire finer foods without artificial chemicals, hormones, and lower quality-of-life conditions. Suddenly what was once a delicious roasted chicken raised on chemicals will smell like a rotting corpse, and you won't be able to put it in your mouth. In the past, you wouldn't have noticed the smell, but now you do. When this happens, you will naturally make a different choice. There is no right or wrong—all reflects levels of consciousness. Water seeks its own level, so it is said.

Q. IS IT TRUE THAT LOCAL HERBS ARE 1,000 TIMES MORE POWERFUL IN THEIR EFFECT THAN HERBS GROWN AWAY FROM US?

A. Not necessarily. Remember that a person is more than a body. You have to consider the soul contract of a person and what they may be karmically working through. For example, let's say I have an illness now living in North Carolina, but maybe the original cause is from some other lifetime in India. It would not be a given that taking herbs grown in North Carolina would affect me better than herbs grown in India. The best course is to follow your own intuition or go to a doctor trained in herbs who is also aware of the effect other lifetimes may have on the cause of illness.

Western Medicine

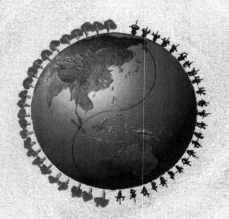

&
Alternative
Therapies

Chapter 5

Western Medicine and Alternative Therapies

Q. WHAT WILL HAPPEN WITH WESTERN MEDICINE VS. ALTERNATIVE MEDICINE IN THE NEAR FUTURE?

A. I'm seeing more artificial methods being used by Western medicine, by which I mean the use of technology that creates artificial solutions—artificial veins, limbs, and organs. Western medicine will think that is a huge breakthrough and that it is just wonderful that they can stimulate cells and program information into cells *electronically* in many ways they couldn't do before.

Western medicine already knows how to clone, but it looks as if there's going to be more technology involved in it. There will be more cloning of organs, but it will still be a while before it will be available to the public.

I'm not seeing that mainstream medicine will move a great deal over to the more holistic view. They seem to be staying in the realm of "technology" science. It is "How can we use science and technology to fix things in people?" I see more sophisticated drugs; some of them feel "electronically charged," which makes me feel very uncomfortable. They will develop drugs that will put electronic messages into the DNA code or into the atoms of our bodies.

So when you ask about the use of holistic or alternative methods, I don't see Western medicine switching from drugs to herbs or homeopathy. Some forms of "energy medicine" and alternative methods will be "allowed" in hospitals and clinics, but it will not be used predominately in Western medicine. Mainstream medicine sees herbs and alternative medicines as methods of the past. There are a few exceptions to this.

Q. IS IT NOT THE CASE THAT HOMEOPATHY AND ALTERNATIVE THERAPIES ARE BEING TAUGHT TO MEDICAL STUDENTS?

A. Even though they are teaching it to students, it is a very small percentage of their education. The *acceptance* of alternative therapies, in comparison to technology, is going to be a very small part of a doctor's repertoire. The training is not geared to produce homeopaths or alternative therapies.
If drugs aren't working, they'll just say they need more research, and we're the guinea pigs. They will usually say, "We just haven't perfected it enough—we just need more time and more funding."

Proportionately, they'll slip in a few alternative therapies such as Reiki and acupuncture, but I still don't see alternative treatments being accepted as a mainstream science.

In many sessions Source has advised us to eat natural foods and use natural remedies whenever possible. It is good to be aware that in Europe they are suddenly trying to make it illegal to practice Homeopathy (ECCH, 2009) even though it's been around since the 1800s. Governments worldwide and some states are trying to control that as well as ban many medicinal herbs, so there is a bit of a witch hunt (Wellness, 2012) going on right now to keep Big Pharma in control to the detriment of all of us.

See "Homeopathy" on page 177.

Q. WILL THERE BE ANY VEILS LIFTED SHOWING SOME OF THE SCAMS THEY'VE BEEN PULLING ON THE AMERICAN PUBLIC?

A. There definitely will be veils lifted, and much truth will be exposed, just as truth is being exposed all over the world now on many levels. You've got to remember that it's mainly about money. There will be more lawsuits due to the detrimental information that will be exposed, but I just don't see that stopping anything. When I look ahead to see if that actually puts a kibosh on some of the deceptive practices they're doing, I don't see it stopping them at this time. The money is still the ruling force in the drug companies.

They'll be certain companies that'll dole out some payments, but the beat goes on. What you're going to see is more lawyer ads on TV that offer suits if you've been harmed by certain drugs. You'll see more of that and people will receive payments, but it still doesn't seem to be enough to put a dent in the pharmaceutical pocket, at least that's the way it looks for the moment. Hopefully this will change.

This is why it behooves all people to begin to take control of their own health. We are all being assisted now by higher frequency energies that have been coming into our planet for a number of years. These energies are stimulating our bodies and our DNA. You may be feeling it as little bursts of illumination similar to a light going on in your mind, where you get an awareness of something you wouldn't have known or thought of previously. Remember that "Like attracts like." Many homeopathic remedies can offset any illness, if given in the right potency.

We know an American homeopath who's been trying to make a homeopathic remedy for the chemical dispersants used in the Gulf oil spill. She wanted to create a homeopathic remedy for it, and the government wouldn't give her the chemical constitution of the dispersants. So I wrote her and said, "The word is the thing. All you have to do is write the words 'chemical dispersants used in the gulf oil spill' on a piece of paper and dowse for the particular potency for a patient and write that on the paper too. Then have the patient put the paper in their sock or bra and 'wear' the remedy. It will still carry the desired vibration effect as a 'physical' remedy." Energetically, the word or phrase *is* the thing. You can also "send" the remedy mentally to them, and that will have an effect also.

Western medicine considers this hocus-pocus, but you are now beginning to understand the power of your minds and learning to think and act as your own authority.

Another homeopath we know asked a question one week about "miasma." He wanted to know if there was a faster way to collapse (or heal) miasmas. Miasma, in homeopathic theory, is a general weakness or predisposition to chronic disease that is transmitted down the generational chain. Examples would be cancer, leprosy, TB, *etc.*, which we carry down through generations. It's a slow process to detox those from a person's system, and they have effects on every level—physical, mental, emotional and spiritual.

Source answered the homeopath's question and said, "Yes, there is a faster way to heal miasmas and it is *potentized forgiveness*." He went to work right away and wrote the word "forgiveness" on a piece of paper, and he then went around to each one of us and dowsed us for what potency of forgiveness we each needed. He made each of us our own forgiveness remedy right then and there. We all "proved" the remedy, and we each had our own unique and very powerful reactions to it. Each week we each got a different potency. This was incredibly powerful! Light and dark; we had a mixture of both reactions, showing us our light and our shadow sides.

When I took the forgiveness remedy the first week, I was euphoric. I was in a state of love and bliss, but the next week I experienced just the opposite. I was hypersensitive to every dark agenda going on. It was right when we got to the U.S. and had to drive to upstate New York. We drove through a hail storm in West Virginia that we just knew was not "natural;" it was an artificially engineered storm. The hail lasted for 45 minutes, and every car and truck got off the road. It *felt* sinister. I've never been through anything like that before. The remedy made me very hypersensitive to the dark agenda, and this also needed to be forgiven, as I was watching my rage surface around it.

This can often happen when you take a remedy and you are "proving" it. You can experience varying extremes of emotion. In the case of the "forgiveness" remedy, we each experienced it very differently. Whether you are euphoric and forgiveness is easy, or you are sensitive to the dark agenda, forgiveness is still what's needed. Experiencing the dark agenda shows the degree of forgiveness needed and also shows how all encompassing it is. How can we really achieve peace if we are all still part of the negative agenda on some level of *our being*? What we experience "out there" is also within us—from extreme light to extreme dark—it is all *us*. We have to be able to forgive the darkest of extremes. This is what the forgiveness remedy was showing us.

What it was also implying was that all of those miasmas were things or events in history that weren't forgiven. We had a member of the group who was a retired university professor. His two biggest issues, in terms of things that repeatedly bothered him, were the holocaust and the potato famine in Ireland. He got his remedy, and in the next week one of his neighbors who hadn't seen him in months stopped in and said to him, "I just had to bring you these *blight-free* potatoes!" Our guy realized it was an instant manifestation from Spirit to let him know that the diseased famine potatoes were now a forgiven thing of the past. He ran into his back yard and planted every one of those blight-free potatoes!

I'm mentioning this to make the point that we don't have to feel limited by conventional medicine, even though it has its place and has saved many lives in emergency situations. There are many ways to heal and strengthen ourselves using our powers of visualization, imagination and true reason, as well as practical things like juicing and eating more live foods. We are living in a live universe of frequency and consciousness, and it can be enhanced and altered by what we *focus* on.

Q. WOULD STEM CELLS BE BENEFICIAL IN HELPING TO KEEP PEOPLE ALIVE LONGER?

A. Yes, and it will lead scientists to discover other benefits of stem cells, which they wouldn't discover if they didn't do this research.

Q. WILL WESTERN MEDICINE EVER FIND A CURE FOR CANCER?

A. Many cures for cancer are known and are being deliberately suppressed by those who are profiting from keeping the cures quiet, namely the pharmaceutical companies.. Researchers know that many cancers can be reduced or reversed through life style change, detoxification, and herbal remedies. Many cancers are related to fungi, environmental pollutants, processed foods and emotional trauma. There are many holistic tools available to help with these issues.

Q. ARE THEY EVER GOING TO TELL US ABOUT THEM, OR USE THEM TO START SAVING LIVES?

A. It's going to come out in increments over the next few years. They'll come out with a piece of information about cancer that they've actually known about for years. They'll act like it's a huge breakthrough, but they won't give you all of the information. They'll give you a little bit to make people say, "Wow! Aren't they doing a tremendous job!"

There are other things involved, because 90% of cancers are due to environmental toxins. If they came out and said that, in terms of the industries involved and the environmental impact it would have on companies who are abusing the environment, it would cause a whole new set of issues to have to be dealt with. There's a whole other piece to this, so that's part of the reason why they'll only give information to the public in small doses.

Q. IS MEDICAL SCIENCE INTERFERING WITH AN INDIVIDUAL'S LIFE PATH OR PLAN WHEN IT KEEPS THEM ALIVE ON A MACHINE?

A. No, because on some level the spirit has agreed to this. It may be to teach something to those involved, or to provide time for some reconciliation on some level. Oftentimes the "patient" on life support is doing things on other spiritual levels while they are unconscious. You really don't know who's learning from the experience or what the opportunities are. There are stories of people who were in comas for years and then came out of it. There are others who die after some time has passed—it really is so individual. The point here is that a person has many levels to them—they are spirit, soul, angel, and many other facets. They have alternate selves in other realities. It isn't as simple as having a physical body with a brain and heart, for example. We are complex beings, and we exist on many levels simultaneously, which is why it is a mistake to assume that we know what is going on with an individual whose life we view strictly from a 3-D physical-awareness perspective.

Think about how things work in this world—there are people who get in horrible accidents who should not survive but do and then somebody else will die over the smallest little thing. When you see this happen, you have to know something greater is operating. In the case of keeping someone alive, if the spirit really wanted to disconnect from its body and leave, it would. The exception to this, of course, is if a person has made their wishes known beforehand that they do not wish to be kept alive by artificial means.

It would be a wonderful advancement in consciousness and medicine if the medical profession were trained in spirituality so they could communicate telepathically with patients who are in comas or unconscious.

We have such limitations in our communication abilities and communion with all life everywhere. We need to stop looking at things separately and inanimately and realize that consciousness continues way beyond the limitations of the physical body and can be accessed through the brain-mind interface or directly from spirit to spirit.

Q. HOW IS THE ASTROLOGICAL CHART AFFECTED FOR A CHILD WHO IS BORN THROUGH CAESARIAN SECTION?

A. It doesn't affect it. A child's birth is in its soul contract and it would be very aware that it will be a caesarian baby. Remember that the soul reincarnating is aware of the time period it is being born into, who the family and parents are, what it is here to do, etc.

Suicide

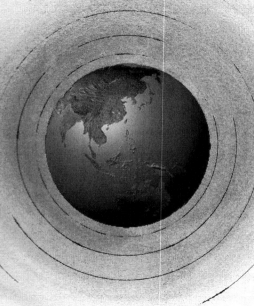

& Mental Illness

Chapter 6

Suicide & Mental Illness

Q. WHAT CHANGES DO YOU SEE IN THIS TIME OF CHANGE REGARDING MENTAL ILLNESSES LIKE SCHIZOPHRENIA?

A. They're explaining that *schizophrenia* is a frequency issue. You may see more of it as things speed up and the veils that hide other planes of existence thin. I wouldn't just call it schizophrenia, in that it is not limited to schizophrenia. It is like a rubber band that gets stretched too thin. As these frequencies come in, some people will be able to integrate these changes well and move through them smoothly, while others will not be able to handle them. You will see more cases of people who can't be stretched any further, and this will be classified medically as a mental illness.

Consider what happens to the nervous system when one gets struck by lightning. How much lightning can a person handle? Some people can handle it relatively well—their body can survive—while other people are totally fried by it and many die. It's the same idea really—the need for more clean water, but it's why fluids are so important electrically for your own body systems.

Q. COULD YOU EXPLAIN MORE ABOUT HOW WE ARE PULLING IN NEGATIVE INTERFERENCE AS A PART OF US?

A. What we perceive as negative interference is information that gets passed around on what looks like little telegraph wires going through the whole planet. Imagine us as in this field or web. If you haven't cleared your own negative perceptions, you will bring in negative interference, depending on where you are at the moment. In other words, like attracts like. Our thoughts attract like energies. Understand that we can quite easily and quickly flip our minds back and forth between positive and negative. What type of field you tune into at any given moment will resonate with where your thoughts and feelings are at the time. Since we are all flipping back and forth all the time between light and dark, if we were to watch our thoughts carefully, we would catch ourselves doing this and could move into more positive thoughts.

Q. What about people who commit suicide?

A. Source makes no judgment around it. It welcomes all spirits. This is important in order to dispel the belief that those who commit suicide go to "hell." That is not to say they go to "heaven" right away either. Where a person who commits suicide finds themselves after death is determined by their own level of consciousness, in that "like attracts like." Everything is consciousness, and each spirit is on an evolutionary journey. It is the spirit that is on the evolutionary journey, not the soul. The soul is the accumulation of what is learned, it is not what's on the journey itself.

Each spirit is in charge of its own consciousness evolution, and the choices and decisions it makes determine its progress or lack thereof through lifetimes. Because we are all in relationship with one another, everyone at the end of each lifetime reviews everything that they have chosen, which includes the effects they have had on others as well as themselves. This is not a judgment process; rather it is a review. However the review shows that no one is an island, and what we do and choose is felt by all life everywhere on some level. Suicide, therefore, is not an escape from oneself ultimately, even though it gets the individual out of their present-life circumstances.

People do have a right to end their contract, to decide for themselves whether or not they're going to continue with their soul plan, but whatever is not learned will have to be learned at some point in their spiritual journey. On the one hand you have all eternity to grow. If your choice is to prolong your learning, you can, but on the other hand, you can't escape it. I realize this is difficult to hear for those who have "lost" others to suicide, and certainly we are not encouraging suicide as an answer for any spirit. Source does love all creations and Its will is happiness.

Q. What happens to the spirit when it crosses over?

A. Each will be having his/her own experience, just like any other spirit who crosses over. Remember "like attracts like," so there is always work to do in spirit, as in form. Those who commit suicide can get stuck quite easily in the astral planes once they cross over because of their level of consciousness at the time they take their lives. I have seen them go to a place of reflection where they reflect on their lives after they have their life review. They will be shown what other choices they could have made. They will be met with love and compassion, like every other spirit who crosses over. Healing will be provided, but it will not erase the need for their own learning. They will be kindly shown areas where other choices and decisions could have produced other outcomes.

Q. DO THEY GO TO PURGATORY?

A. There is no actual place called purgatory but its idea represents spirits that get stuck in the astral planes. All types of spirits can get stuck here, not just those who take their lives, which is why it is appropriate to continue to pray for the deceased to offer them love or forgiveness so they are able to go to the Light. Not all souls go to the Light right away, but most do.

Q. IS IT STILL CONSIDERED SUICIDE IF A PERSON IS SICK, HAS NO QUALITY OF LIFE AND TAKES THEIR OWN LIFE?

A. Yes, the person is still ending his/her contract before it is up naturally, and the person could have been burning off a karmic debt.

Q. WHEN A PERSON COMMITS SUICIDE, THERE IS OFTEN VIOLENCE INVOLVED. WOULD ANY HOMEOPATHIC REMEDY HELP A SPIRIT ONCE THEY CROSS?

A. You would handle it just as you would any other person who is coming to you. If you were going to deal with it on the level of spirit, you must be able to talk to the spirit first. You have to take the case just as you would any individual. There is no general remedy that would apply in these cases.

Q. IS IT TRUE THAT PEOPLE WHO COMMIT SUICIDE HAVE DONE IT BEFORE IN OTHER LIFETIMES?

A. There can be a repeat pattern for some of these spirits who continually find their lessons on the Earth too difficult, but it isn't true for all those who take their lives. Many of these souls are learning how to have perseverance and courage, or how to overcome adversity, or how to know their innate self worth. They will continue to reincarnate until they succeed.

Some people commit suicide because of chemical imbalances that make their journey especially hard. Some also are here to try to clear ancestral karma, which is a heavy karmic load dealing with generations past and future. Suicide is seen as an act of honor in certain cultures. The point is that all spirits return to the Earth to continue their evolution, and they will have the opportunity to choose a higher road next time. Is suicide the best way? Probably not, but that is the individual's choice.

Working with homeopathic color remedies can help people who often feel suicidal. Many carry too much or too little of certain colors in their biologies.

Ultimately, it's always about forgiveness, but people are at different stages in their spiritual evolution and need to be treated at the level that they can integrate and accept.

Q. IS EUTHANASIA THE SAME AS SUICIDE?

A. Yes, if the individual is asking for it consciously. We need to remember that for a spirit to become masterful, it faces challenges and needs to acquire virtues. Its choices have a huge effect on its evolution. If you opt out of a lifetime early because you say you can't hack it, there's no judgment from Source about it, but at some point in your spiritual journey you will need to master your challenges. Source is a God of Love, and Love will always desire to bring you into its full awareness.

We have to be very careful here. It would be presumptuous to be a part of helping someone end his or her life. This would create karma between all those involved, because it would bind them in a spirit decision that should only be done by the individual spirit. The exception to this, of course, is if a person has made their wishes known beforehand that they do not wish to be kept alive by artificial means.

Q. WOULD THIS BE THE SAME WHEN WE EUTHANIZE AN ANIMAL?

A. No karma is created when we euthanize an animal when the animal is in pain and our intentions are to relieve suffering. The reason is that animals are not conscious choosers as are humans and they do not make soul contracts the way humans do. We would create karma for ourselves, if we were destroying an animal for convenience purposes.

Q. IF WE COULD FINE TUNE OUR VISION OF SUICIDE, MIGHT WE SEE THAT THE PERSON'S LEAVING WAS NECESSARY ON THE TRANSPERSONAL LEVEL?

A. Rarely, there are cases in which the leaving could be necessary on the transpersonal level. Still, there would be so much unknown in these cases that it would not be wise to assume this is what's happening. In most cases of suicide, it is not necessary that the spirit leave—it is a choice made from a painful state of consciousness.

Q. IS A PERSON'S DECISION TO LEAVE EVER IN CONCERT WITH THE NATURAL LAWS OF SOURCE, OR IS IT ALWAYS A WILLFUL DECISION OF THE INDIVIDUAL WHICH RESULTS IN KARMA?

A. The natural law of Source is Life and Love. A person who commits suicide is not in a place of Love if they are ending their own life. There is no judgment in suicide, so no karma is created. The karma exists where the spirit's challenges are not worked through and will be met again in another lifetime. There is no original soul contract for suicide—in other words, it is not a pre-ordained destiny. It is always a decision by each individual in his or her 3-D life. We are not calling it a willful decision because the person committing suicide is not in his/her true will.

It must be realized that every spirit is here to mature its soul in some way. Many spirits don't fulfill their soul contracts, and most do not take their own lives. Reincarnation occurs because of things left unfinished, unresolved and yet to be realized. Every spirit ultimately will achieve Self- or God-realization, but it may take an indeterminable number of incarnations to achieve this mastery. The spirit of the one committing suicide is no exception to this process. The choices we make in each lifetime either further our soul progress or set it back. Either way, we are the ones who are in relationship with ourselves, and there is no escaping from this fact. Mary Engelbright said it well, "Wherever you go, there you are." This is actually joyous news, when you understand that you are in charge of your own path and you are afforded many opportunities to progress. God Source is Love.

A person commits suicide because they believe their life will never get better or they perceive themselves in too much pain to continue this life. They are unable to see how things will be different, and they desire to be free of the pain as they perceive it. Some do it in a time of desperation or anger, and many do have regret, once they are shown in spirit the value of life

Q. WHAT IS THE LOVING MESSAGE THAT A PERSON WHO COMMITS SUICIDE WOULD WANT TO GIVE TO DEVASTATED SURVIVORS?

A. Most spirits who commit suicide want forgiveness first and foremost. Most say they are sorry to those left behind. They are not always sorry for committing suicide—they are sorry for the confusion, guilt and devastation it may have caused those left behind. They always indicate that no one else is the cause or at fault for their decision. They readily admit self-responsibility in the act. That they can communicate these things to those left behind proves they are not in hell. They all go through a life review, just as any soul crossing over would do. They face themselves as any other soul would. They see the good in their life as well as the difficulties, the successes as well as the failures. The difficulties or failures remain to be reconciled at another time, and they can learn and realize much while in the spirit world.

Q. WHAT IS IT LIKE FOR THEM TO LEAVE THEIR BODY IN THIS WAY? WOULD THEY DO IT DIFFERENTLY NEXT TIME?

A. Leaving the body is almost always a joyous release, and most find it a release from struggle while others may be stuck in the astral planes. The exception for normal deaths would be those who die suddenly and unexpectedly through an accident or other surprise circumstances. Sometimes those spirits find themselves disoriented and unable to accept that they have died. There can be a period before these spirits completely go to the Light. Prayers for *all* who pass is always a good practice.

Q. HOW CAN DEPRESSED PEOPLE CHOOSE TO STAY POSITIVE WHEN THEY DON'T HAVE ENOUGH ENERGY TO DO SO?

A. A person who is feeling depressed is feeling in effect of their world and what is or isn't occurring within it. They may also be carrying imprints from other lifetimes with them into their current life. Consider the state of depression as a stagnant state of being where the person is feeling paralyzed or hopeless to change their environment or their lives. When you have a great amount of energy that is stuck or stagnant, it wears on the will of the individual and causes fatigue. Therefore, an unraveling process must be initiated and can be initiated on a variety of levels. This can be done through journaling about your feelings - being very self honest with yourself, exercise, breathing techniques, yoga, walking, meditating, cranio-sacral therapy, past life regression, and soul retrievals, for example. Other ways are the use of medicines designed to change brain chemistry, which work on the physical level, and does temporarily alter brain patterns although using these most likely will not remove the cause of the depression but they may give you sufficient reprieve in order to begin the unraveling process mentioned above.

All depression is a feeling of powerlessness on some level and requires added self-discovery. Related to it is an element of denial of one's reality, or the desire to deny some aspect of it. The act of *de-pressing* is to keep something below the level of conscious or current reality. Exploring what is being denied or suppressed can oftentimes free the energy to move on and out. Different choices will most likely need to be made by the individual.

A person can also choose each day to invite their Paradise self to become active within their biology as well as to be willing to let go of all their previous beliefs about themselves. Although this sounds simplistic, the invitation to one's Paradise self will begin to move old stagnant energies out and will inspire new ideas or solutions.

See "Q. Is a person who is considering suicide ready to relinquish all experiences?" on page 145. Also see "Suicides" on page 177.

Food & Water

Chapter 7

Food and Water

Q. WHAT'S HAPPENING TO OUR FOOD SUPPLY?

A. You'll never have a *shortage* of food—that's not the NA's game. The game is to raise the price of food so you can't buy as much. Things will be delivered to where they need to be, but the prices are going up due to fuel prices rising, droughts, and storms that may cause delays in shipments.

Q. WHAT ABOUT GENETICALLY MODIFIED FOOD?

A. Genetically modified (GMO) food is well underway—it's just a fact that it's happening. (WHO, 2012) These foods could make you ill—they can affect your digestion. Avoid the soybeans and corn and anything made from them. Genetically modified corn can make men sterile, which many of us have been reading about (Technology, 2009). The feed they are giving animals is genetically modified, which affects the quality of their milk, eggs and meat. (*ibid.*)

If you can buy organic, do so, because I see the digestive systems of people changing from consuming GMO foods and not being able to cope with the artificial aspects of genetically modified foods. Liver disease and stomach disorders can be the effects of these artificially engineered foods. There is a strong movement towards eating foods that are organic and grown locally, which shows people are following their inner guidance.

(See also "Food Labeling" on page 177.)

Q. WHAT ABOUT OUR WATER?

Source wants us to know that water is going to be very important. It's very important that you all have filtered water. It is very important for you to get your water clean, have plenty of it, and drink lots of it, because you have to keep up with the rate at which this influx of Light is coming in. You have to keep good circulation going on in and through your body. Charge your water by putting prayers into your water, or tone colors into water, especially the color green. Do not drink tap water unless it is well water that you know is pure. You should have a water filter in your car (even if it is small) in case you get stuck somewhere.

We all need plenty of pure, clean water, and the water of the planet is asking us for conscious prayer. You can do it with your own glass of water because all water is connected to all water. The trees themselves have asked us this before in another session where they were upset about what's happening to the *quality* of water that's coming up through their roots. They are not happy that their ability to give us oxygen is being thwarted. So include the trees in your intentions when you focus on your water. You don't have to do anything drastic, get yourself a filter, and make your prayer into every glass of water you drink because the water is asking for it.

The oceans especially are asking for conscious prayer. Be conscious of the water in your body as well. Send it loving thoughts, and do a fast or cleanse every six months.

Remember that water holds the imprint and memory of what's around it, which includes what is *said* in its vicinity. It will either hold the imprint or memory of positive surroundings or negative ones. Think about that as you drink it!

What or who, has the water in your glass been around? What did it hear or record? That is what you are drinking and what your body will materialize. This is the same with the food you eat—what do you inherit from the foods you eat?

What the oceans are showing me is that if something was polluting the air, Mother Nature would do her purifying rain. This would be her normal cycle of nature, in much the same way as our bodies eliminate what is not good for us. It's a little bit more complex than that now for the Earth, because she can't keep up.

The pollutants that are going into her system now are so toxic that she can't keep up with the demand for purifying it. The fact that the NA is orchestrating false storms and sending unhealthy pulses through the oceans is not helping. But you can do a lot.

The waters are saying this: "One molecule is all molecules." Talk to the water in your body as well—it represents the waters of the Earth—make a deliberate intention for purification. We all need to drink a lot more pure water than we have been.

Artificially Engineered Viruses

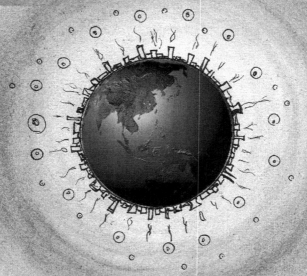

Chapter 8

Artificially Engineered Viruses

Participant: "I attended a high-level government meeting once to which I happened to get invited accidentally. I shouldn't have really been there, however I found myself there. The seating arrangement was very tightly controlled as to who sat beside whom. Military honors were going on for veterans returning from Iraq.

"I was seated at a table of scientists, and the woman seated next to me just happened to say to me in conversation, 'It's just like when we created the AIDS virus in Africa.' I said sheepishly, 'Can you expand on that a little?' and she went on to explain how 'they' created the AIDS virus and put this fantastic façade on it that it was a disease caused by homosexuality. They were pretending to find a cure for it.

"I came out of there in total shock, but what was even more surprising was that everybody else around the table already knew that. I was the only one that didn't know it. This was common knowledge to all of them."

Q. WHAT ELSE WERE THEY PLANNING?

A. They have created artificial strains of the flu virus. These are viruses that are not organic or natural. I don't know what else to say about it except that you *don't need a vaccine for them.* Let's understand that, vaccines are actually a way of weakening your system and getting the virus *into* your system. Be very cautious and discriminating concerning vaccines—especially for your children, young girls, the elderly, and of course, yourselves. Better to keep your immune system strong by natural methods or the use of homeopathy, color therapy, live foods or herbs when needed. Your immune system doesn't need to deal with artificially produced poisons masquerading as a virus threat.

Take care and look after yourself. Each one of you has been given *your* body to look after—to keep the balance.

Q. IS THE SWINE FLU PROJECT STILL ACTIVELY PURSUED BY THE GOVERNMENT AT THIS TIME?

A. Yes, indeed.

Q. ARE VACCINES BENEFICIAL AT ALL?

A. No inoculations are really beneficial. They all introduce poisonous elements into your system.

Dr. Viera Scheibner is a retired micropaleontologist and leading researcher in the anti-vaccination field. She has been writing and lecturing about vaccination since her study in the 1980s of babies' stress-induced breathing patterns introduced her to the subject and led her to collect and study more than 100,000 pages of medical papers on vaccination. Her conclusion is that "100 years of orthodox research shows that vaccines represent a medical assault on the immune system."

(For more information on the danger of vaccinations, see "Vaccinations" on page 180.)

Q. IS THE PLAN TO MICROCHIP EACH PERSON A POSITIVE THING?

A. I have a feeling of sorrow from Source about that. Microchips interfere with the circuitry of the whole being, so "no," it is not a positive thing and is a plan of the NA.

Earth

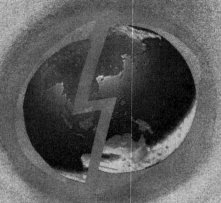

Changes

Chapter 9

Earth Changes

Since 2010 I have been asked what will occur specifically in Earth changes. I have reported what I have seen each time to the groups, and those events have manifested. However, because the Earth grids change daily as the consciousness of the people changes, I no longer make specific predictions for a few reasons. We are in a fluctuating field, and the grids of the Earth are in a state of flux.

We have also seen through these transcripts that the NA likes to use *us* to create cataclysmic changes. For this reason, I feel it is best not to predict specific events—in this way we can avoid any of us giving them energy and causing them to manifest. Source has made it clear that cataclysmic events are *not* a prerequisite for growth and change but occur due to imbalances within a planetary system. "Weeding out" or "cleansing" only happens when the consciousness of a planet has been stuck on a descending wheel for too long.

Q. I SENSE IN THE VERY NEAR FUTURE THAT THERE COULD BE MAJOR FINANCIAL SHIFTS, OR OTHER GLOBAL SHIFTS. IS THAT SOMETHING THAT'S IN THE WORKS?

A. Financially, that is all being manipulated. In the U.S.A., the powers that be are going to soften the effects of their orchestration of a collapse until the elections of 2012 are over.

In other words, any sort of a catastrophic financial event is being delayed for the moment. They want our economy to appear to be getting better. So you're actually going to hear and see reports where things seem to be improving. It's part of the global orchestration. That will get us a little bit of a reprieve temporarily.

2013 is going to be interesting. The mass consciousness of the people will determine how many events unfold. In terms of what we're all creating for

2012, there will be moments where the powers that be will use the consciousness of the people to give them a little bit of what they expect. There are many who expect an Armageddon, and the NA just might use that to actually orchestrate some *symptoms* of it. We all need to look carefully at our global *Earth change* expectations for our future and make decisions for a new Golden Age instead of for an Armageddon.

Source is saying: "I am benign. I do not cause catastrophic events in your world." Source's energy is peace, and It wants well-being for everyone and everything, everywhere. Source is *not* orchestrating catastrophes now or *ever*. Source needs that said right up front. *Choose* this truth, despite what we are being told otherwise.

You're going to hear all kinds of things as we move into the new Golden Age after 2012. Source's intention for the world is that it be a Golden Age, or "Paradise." But it's up to *us* to choose that.

The truth is that we are in a cycle; the Earth is moving; things are moving; wheels within wheels are moving in the cosmos; gates are opening and closing; new frequencies of Light are coming in, and we are waking up. This moment is for more light to come in, not for any kind of devastation. Let's all get on line with that and dismiss whatever is negative as orchestrations from ill-intentioned people.

There's no reason we can't have a smooth accelerated awakening into more of our true presence, which is what this time of change is designed to do.

After the 2012 election is over, you'll see the NA start to mess around again. You'll see periods of coasting along with some upheaval just to make us all happy.

Q. DO YOU SEE A MASS SHIFT IN CONSCIOUSNESS COMING, AS IN THE HUNDREDTH-MONKEY SYNDROME?

A. The hundredth monkey refers to the idea that if enough consciousness is moved into a certain awareness, it will pull the rest of the mass consciousness with it. A critical mass of energy carries the rest, if you will.

You will continue to see accelerating quantum leaps in awareness. The Occupy Wall Street and other sovereignty movements are really waking up people. Their methods are exposing a lot of things coming. They are uprooting old perceptions in many people who have been hanging onto certain traditions and dogmas for too long. That's going to increase; you'll see more and more of that around the world—more and more demonstrations, more truths being exposed. So, yes, there's a huge quantum shift happening.

Q. WILL THIS GOLDEN TIME CHANGE OUR COLLECTIVE CONSCIOUSNESS?

A. Yes, but it's got to be an awakening *within the individual*, which is why the demonstrations on Wall Street and around the world are actually good things. Will it actually shift the *politics* around the world? That process feels like muck to me, in the sense that the process will be neither easy nor instant.

It's the same answer as the money, the pharmaceutical industry and the politics. Their particular system has been in control for so long and involves so many countries, that any shift in that system is going to be very slow.

Again, the bigger picture is that these efforts are waking people up. Once the truth begins to emerge, the public is going to want more of it. They're going to listen now to more truths. First it's going to be the truth about the corruption in the financial institutions, and then it's going to be the medical establishment, the drug companies and the whole witch hunt against holistic and alternative health care. Trying to put bans on herbs is another corruption. You'll see a huge revolt before too long. You're going to see a progression of "we the people" standing up for human rights and personal freedoms.

Q. WE NOW HAVE SEVEN BILLION PEOPLE IN THE WORLD. DO YOU SEE WORLD POPULATION DECLINING AT ALL?

A. That's a very diplomatic question. You will see people leave the planet. You will see groups of people leave the planet in events. There may be one or two major events in 2012 depending on how we manifest balance, but you will see there are actually a lot of souls who want out of here now. Many have contracted to leave at this time. So you will see people come and go, but what I hear Source saying is "But you've always seen that."

There have always been people and souls coming and going. If you are asking about the NA's depopulation agenda, there's going to be a bit of a halt to that. Part of it is because people are wising up to the NA's plan, and it is not always wise to cause such wide-scale catastrophe in an election year.

Also, I've heard from others that the NA who *were* orchestrating this population-control scheme have been confronted by a covert and very powerful group of people who are threatening to take them out if they proceed with their depopulation agenda and I received confirmation from Source to share it.

Source says things are being rethought and reorchestrated so that the momentum that we all heard about for depopulation seems to have been slowed. Source wants us to know that there are *so many* new advanced souls coming into this planet right now that there's a line of them waiting to come in.

Source says, "Don't think I am unaware of what's happening—do you really think those 'little minions' can destroy my creation?"

Q. DOES A ONE-WORLD GOVERNMENT ON PLANET EARTH FIT IN WITH GOD'S PLAN?

A. These are the affairs of men, and God is not involved in it. Source reveals it is not in Its Plan. It goes against the laws of free will and the eternal-life principle.

Q. WHY DOES THE GOVERNMENT WANT TO TAKE GOD OUT OF EVERYTHING? WHO IS REALLY BEHIND THIS?

A. The NA wants us to go even deeper into forgetting that we are created by God Source. They are taking the word "God" out of public arenas so you won't be hearing the word "God" every day. They would like the word "God" to be heard less and less in people's hearing range as part of the "artificializing" process. However, there is nothing stopping us from repeating the name of God daily and energizing it in our daily lives and affirming that God Source *lives within* us. Do not forget that you are God in action in this physical world.

Q. WERE THE AMERICAN FOUNDING FATHERS FROM THE SAME
GALACTIC SOUL FAMILY?

A. No, they were from varying Star Systems who came together for a distinct soul purpose of establishing the principles of freedom and self-sovereignty in America. Many of them still work in spirit to uphold this trust.

It is obvious then, from this information, that Source has a desire for our world to progress in a positive and enlightened direction. It is providing us with Light codes and new beings to assist us in this waking up process. It is *we* who have to "take the Light and run with it," so to speak, to have this new reality *anchor* here.

Remember you are alive because you have God within you.

Solar Flares

&
Technology

Chapter 10

Solar Flares & Technology

Q. WITH THE SOLAR FLARES THAT ARE AFFECTING THE ELECTRO-MAGNETIC FIELD OF THIS PLANET, I HAVE NOTICED PROBLEMS WITH COMPUTER AND PHONE TECHNOLOGY. SOMETIMES I PICK UP MY PHONE AND PEOPLE CAN'T HEAR ME OR I CAN'T HEAR THEM. EVERYONE I'M TALKING TO IS HAVING ISSUES. MY QUESTION IS: IS IT GOING TO GET WORSE BEFORE IT GETS BETTER?

A. There are technicians who are working on technology now that will be able to lessen the effect of solar flares on computer systems and satellites. It's a work in progress to create shielding. You're going to experience the effects of solar flares on technology for a while—it's just the way it's going to be. In 2013 they will have developed something that will be shielding some of these effects. So there's technology in progress.

Q. WE JUST HAD SOME INTENSE SUN SPOT ACTIVITY AND THE ASTRONOMERS ARE SAYING WE'RE GOING INTO A VERY HEAVY ACTIVITY PERIOD THAT'S GOING TO LAST 3-5 YEARS. WHAT EFFECT WILL THEY HAVE ON OUR COMMUNICATION SYSTEMS?

A. The Sun is being acted upon by forces beyond itself, as are other planets in the cosmos and other galaxies as well. Only part of it is coming from within the Sun—the other part is coming from deeper in the cosmos. In terms of its effect on us and our communications, yes, you will see communications disrupted on many levels—computers, satellites, increasing geomagnetic storms, *etc.*

We are very dependent on our technologies. However, we all have it built into our cellular structure to be telepathic with one another. There's no excuse for us not to be practicing telepathy with one another so that our ability to send messages and communicate isn't solely dependent on outside sources.

Seriously, with the Earth changes that we're in, do practice communicating with each other using telepathy. It would be wonderful to create a group that has a project and has weekly experiments to send messages to one another—to your children who are out of the state or country, to people, relatives and friends around the world. If something occurred where you couldn't talk to these people, you can send them thoughts and they'd get the message.

Q. WHAT ARE OTHER WAYS WE CAN PRACTICE TELEPATHY?

A. You can practice with your automobile or with your animals and plants or with affecting your own body. These are all consciousness. There are people who have turned on their cars with their minds or reversed illnesses. When we talk about self-mastery we talk about it on a variety of levels, and the mental level is an aspect of mastery. Everything around you is living and conscious. You are in relationship with it; make it your business to get to know it.

Q. ARE WE GIVING UP OUR FREE WILL BY USING COMPUTERS AND CELL PHONES, AND RELYING ON THEM?

A. Let's put it this way: Any time you've got your hands on a keyboard, every time you hold a telephone to your ear, you are hooking up to a low-frequency energy field without knowing the ramifications of that. You are not consciously giving up your free will because you don't know how harmful technology can be to your bodies and immune systems. But without knowing, the more you are exposing yourself to those fields, the more it is weakening your body and altering its organic cellular structure.

The water in our bodies is "stagnant" in comparison to the water in a "resurrected" body. Low-frequency technology, artificial foods, *etc.*, weaken the water in your body and destroy its organic crystalline structure.

Q. SHOULD WE CUT BACK ON USAGE OF COMPUTERS AND CELL PHONES?

A. It is suggested that instead of using artificial technology, we connect with the crystals in our own body.

Q. WHAT DOES THIS MEAN?

A. It means that the crystals in your body have their own organic information system. We need to remember that we are made up of crystals. Our very biology is crystals. Instead of us thinking that we need to rely on artificial intelligence for communication, it would be much better if we started to use the communication system within our own body.

People who are really clear about telepathic communication understand it is coming from their own body. You are connected to an information system already by the fact that these crystals make up your biology. It would behoove us all to rely more on our own internal intelligence for communication than to rely so much on external devices. It is not saying that you never need a computer to type a letter or do your business. However, taking the time to activate and use your own telepathic crystal network is a good idea.

Q. HOW CAN WE PROTECT OURSELVES?

A. The more of your true organic self you merge with, the more natural immunity you will have to lower frequencies and pulses.

Increase your intake of Vitamin C. Practice forgiveness and self-forgiveness daily.

Put a rubber cover over your computer keyboard or visualize orange light over the keyboard and monitor. Use the "hands free" device when using cell phones.

Implement EMF screening strategies in your home and workplace.

Technology is a reversal of our organic true self. In fact, if you were to be fearful of anything, be fearful of technology. The NA's plan is to integrate a very low frequency into our physical bodies so that we lose the ability to be our organic true selves or achieve resurrection.

The NA knows that our DNA is changing with the influx of higher frequencies onto this planet. We are beginning to remember our true selves, and our higher senses are awakening. The NA plan on using the nerve network in our solar plexus and naval chakras to interfere with our awakening by altering our biology through pulsing, genetically modified foods, biological weaponry and genetically modified trees.

The NA knows that using our solar plexus and navel chakras allows them to plug into everybody on the planet as a unit. We are all linked to each other and to the electromagnetic web around the Earth from these chakras. Their plan is to use technology and artificial products to alter our solar plexus and naval chakras in order to control the whole electromagnetic web around the Earth *through us*.

They are fueling it through the energy of our bodies because we are all interconnected—not only to one another, but to the web. In other words, *we* are the power source for them to put forward their agenda. Genetically modified foods are digested in our stomach and intestines, weakening us and making us more "artificial." It is very important that we do not allow our solar plexus to become corded with their artificial intelligence. This is the point where the NA tries to destroy our organic humanity.

We need to understand that the energy web created by the interrelationship between all of us is enormously powerful—so powerful it can cause catastrophes or miraculous events. The negative agenda is aware of this. When they send pulses of very low frequencies into this energy web it causes us to have very low thoughts and feelings.

In this way, our own negative thoughts and feelings create events of like kind in our world. If we knew this, we could turn the tables on them and send out miraculous thoughts and feelings. You can develop this ability and utilize this energy web by realizing that it is your solar plexus that has the ability to connect to the world web—not the computer web—but the world web around the planet. We can each send very different messages—positive messages, miraculous messages. Better yet, by being our true organic selves, we will automatically be a miraculous, radiating force.

This is what the negative agenda does not want us to find out—they want to use our energy systems to create cataclysms and disasters through low frequency fears, thoughts and emotions so they remain in control. It is *we* who are doing the creating through our bodies *for* them and haven't realized how this is working. Now that we are being made aware of how this works, we can consciously project miraculous thoughts out into the world web through our solar plexus nerve network. This way we can't be used for any negative agenda.

Earth and
The Ending of
Evil

Chapter 11

Earth and the Ending of Evil

Q. WILL THE MAGNETIC FIELD OF THE EARTH REVERSE?

A. It is already reversing and has been for a number of years. Many airports have changed their runways to accommodate this change in the Earth's magnetic field. Magnetic reversals are common and have occurred throughout Earth's history.

Q. WILL THERE BE A POLE SHIFT?

A. There will be a spin reversal. The poles will not flip, but the spin direction is changing.

Q. WHAT DOES THAT MEAN FOR US AS A POPULATION, AND DOES THIS COINCIDE WITH THE PROPHECIES ABOUT THE END OF THE WORLD?

A. There is going to be a separation of those who do not desire to change compared to those that are going to shift cooperatively. This separation actually feels good and it is important and necessary. You are going to see a division, a separation between those that would enslave and those that would be free. The forces of evil are going to be separated out from those that are upholding the Life Principle. Many of us are going to be in this wonderful, wonderful advancement. There is a spin coming, but the spin is a purifying spin.

Q. ARE THERE COSMIC RAYS OR A HIGHER ENERGY FORM THAT IS CAUSING THIS?

A. Don't think of it in those small terms. In other words, gamma rays or things coming off the cosmos are only a diluted version of what is behind it. What is behind it goes beyond all of that and is much bigger. This is coming from Source. Like the Beings that are coming towards us, it is a force that is coming toward us. This force is disconnecting the cords of evil that have been holding people in bondage for many centuries.

I now understand where they get the term "the rapture" because when I see people being cleared of these things, I see ecstasy, a huge expansion of consciousness when we finally get to know what God and "we" are. Finally!

Q. WHAT WILL THIS LOOK LIKE ON A 3-D LEVEL?

As I said before, predictions help manifest an outcome and I am choosing not to contribute to these manifestations. What I am willing to report is the answer below.

A. There will be some cataclysmic events in this process. You will see waters change, fires, earthquakes, volcanoes, crazy storms, and things topsy-turvy, but from Source's point of view it's just a "shake-up." It is to clean. It wouldn't be necessary if we were more harmonious in our consciousness. Shake-ups occur because we have purification to do as a species due to our imbalances.

The forces of evil are done and will have to leave here. It is a 20-year process from now when this is going to be occurring. You will see many things change and after that, everyone and everything will be different. The Earth will be new. Everything will have shifted to a higher level. Of course, in this 20-year process, we can lessen the impact of these events by coming into balance within ourselves, which will project itself out into the world.

Q. EVEN ANIMALS, PLANTS AND TREES?

A. When I look at animals, plants and trees, all of them are much more violet in aura after the change. Our own blood crystals will be spinning faster with more light in them. We are in a time of cleansing and purification. Our true selves are coming towards us to merge with us.

Q. IS THERE ANY WAY TO AVOID GOING THROUGH THE CHANGES?

A. No, we all have to go through this cleansing. It is necessary for us to come to a more cooperative way of thinking, living and being. In a way, you could say we each need to cleanse our own darkness and come into unity within ourselves. If we don't, it will turn to illness within us. When it is said that those that are here after the changes will be different, it means they will be more aligned to their true selves. It will be a more cooperative world.

Q. THE CONCEPT OF EARTH CHANGES HAS AN ELEMENT OF FEAR IN IT IN REGARDS TO THE FORM OR TYPES OF EARTH CHANGES. ARE YOU SEEING THAT IF WE ALIGN OURSELVES WITH OUR TRUE SELVES, ALL OF THE CHANGE WILL BE GOOD?

A. In the big picture, the Earth changes are good in their goal. But the process of the changes may not always be comfortable. In the big hologram, what is happening is the cleansing. Not everyone is going to experience it as this great, wonderful process, although we could if we can allow ourselves to release our past and move into our true selves. Some may make their transition during this process. How each will experience it has to do with their own individual soul contracts and their state of consciousness.

Q. SHOULD WE BE PUTTING UP STORES/FOOD SUPPLIES?

A. It is important to have pure water and food, not out of a sense of fear but out of a sense of practicality. We are obviously in Earth and climatic changes. However, the more we merge with our true selves who are coming towards us, the more we will be fed spiritually.

Remember, we will naturally desire lighter foods and liquids. Consider being fed by the colors in the atmosphere and the sun, but please note that not all can do this, and it is a highly personal practice, so use caution and discernment. We will all be going through our own purification as we evolve to a higher level of being. Purification is not a punishment. It is part of the process when life forms are moving to a higher level of consciousness.

We will be presented with many options. Some will say "Come and do this" while someone else will say "Go and do that" and so on. You may find yourself a bit overwhelmed with all the choices. Bring all your decisions to your true self who is coming towards you and wait in silence for a thought, feeling or sensation. This is known as silent prayer. You will always feel a sense of inner strength and peace when an answer is coming from your true self.

Q. HOW CAN WE AS A SOCIETY DEAL WITH THE TURMOIL AND THINGS THAT ARE CHANGING IN THE WORLD, AND HOW CAN WE MAKE IT THROUGH IN A POSITIVE WAY WITHOUT FALLING PREY TO THE NEGATIVE AGENDA?

A. A huge infusion of white light came in with that question. The Earth is receiving a frequency of white light that it has never had before. You're going to see many things continue to change, but this is part of the cleansing.

It has been destined to occur now, in this time period. In terms of fear, what you're really asking me is how to not be afraid. We've gone through change before at other time periods—this isn't the first time for many of us. There were family members that we tried to save at other periods that we couldn't save. There is this soul memory that is making us a little apprehensive about the success of this whole process this time around and even the success of ourselves in it. I'm seeing chess pieces on a chess board and how they all get moved around in the game—you're going to see a lot of people moved around in the game, some will fall and get knocked down and some will move to the other side.

This is just part of the roles that each person has—everybody is in their right place doing their right thing. It isn't your responsibility to worry about what happens to everyone. Take care of your spirit; take care of what's in your immediate environment, your family, your community. That's the part you play because you wouldn't be here in this place, in this spot, if you weren't supposed to be taking care of what is in your environment.

Personal intuition will keep increasing on the planet to the point where you'll see people get stronger signals for themselves. They'll get strong feelings if they are to move or do something specific with their lives. You're going to be guided, and you're going to know. The main message is not to have so much fear around this—this is part of a plan that's already in motion.

This white light that is coming in is helping everybody prepare and move to where they're supposed to be.

A lot of the evil that you see going on is because it's time for it to go, so you have to trust that. You also have to trust that if certain people leave this planet, that's the path they've chosen.

Q. SOME OF THE FUTURISTIC TYPE PROGRAMS ARE TALKING ABOUT A SPECIFIC NA GROUP THAT IS TRYING TO TAKE OVER THE WORLD AND MAKE IT A ONE-WORLD GOVERNMENT. CAN YOU COMMENT ON THAT?

A. Yes, that plan is going to collapse.

Q. THAT'S WHAT I'M ASKING—DOES THE NA HAVE THE CAPABILITY TO SUCCEED IN THEIR TAKEOVER PLAN EVEN THOUGH WE HAVE THE FREEDOM OF CHOICE?

A. No, it's predestined that it will fail. It will not succeed to the degree that people fear. The understanding I'm being given is that the time for evil is up.

In Ireland there are many legends about gods and goddesses. There's a particular burial mound that is the tomb of a Celtic warrior queen—Queen Maeve. Whenever I've climbed up to this mound, I could feel the energy of her there very strongly. However, when we went up there in 2011 her energy was gone. I asked Source what had happened—where did she go? I saw these wheels-within-wheels turning in the universe, and this queen was on one of them. It wasn't just her—there were many old gods and goddesses on these wheels also. They were leaving the planet because their time had come to go. If you think about it, the time period of gods and goddesses centered on bloodshed and battles, conquests over others for land and possessions. Curses and spells were the norm. The time for that type of consciousness is over!

There are star-gate openings that are occurring now in the cosmos that are allowing those beings in spirit to go back to where they came from so long ago—before they came in to this planet Earth thousands of years ago.

It is the same thing with evil. It has a deadline to leave this planet, which is why you're seeing things beef up; you're seeing their last-ditch effort to take as many souls with them as they possibly can. Don't fall prey to their negativity or pulsing. Guard your thoughts, feelings and intentions, and stay positive.

With this influx of white light everyone is being awakened on many different levels. There's a cleansing that's going on collectively and personally within each individual. It's like pouring pure water into a glass with sand and it's all being stirred up. Keep your focus on the truth in terms of where we're really headed.

Q. KNOWING THAT RESPONSIBILITY IS AN INDIVIDUAL THING, WHAT RESPONSIBILITY DO WE HAVE TO ASSIST IN RELIEVING THE PAIN AND SUFFERING IN OTHER COUNTRIES IN THE WORLD?

A. I'm going to deal with the responsibility issue first. In this world drama the reason you see things being played out in certain ways is that there are soul contracts and soul agreements and people are at different levels of learning as souls. Some people can be very young or very stubborn in their soul growth. Source allows each soul to take as long as they want to grow and change and there isn't any judgment in Source about it. They could take a million lifetimes and still not take personal responsibility for their thoughts and actions. It really isn't any of our business to worry about that because Source doesn't judge it.

Every soul will choose to wake up eventually, because every soul will want to go Home at some point. We have to respect that everybody is at different levels of their awakening. The difference in this current time period is that all are being stimulated by cosmic forces, and waking up is being catalyzed by these forces. There may still be those who choose not to flow with these changes, and that is their right.

Concerning our responsibilities to other countries, remember it's a collective movement. In other words, it's the people a country is made up of, not the governments.

It's not really about us being responsible for another country, at least on that level, because the collective energy of a place will affect its experience in the world. The best thing anybody can do again is to pay attention to the "place" you are in and tend your own garden. That is your responsibility. That is your contribution. It doesn't mean we never give to another country and vice-versa—but responsibility is an individual process that we are all involved in.

If you feel prompted, you can use your minds to visualize countries receiving what they need; don't wait for your government to do it. It's that old saying that if you know somebody's starving, give them a loaf of bread, you don't give them a bunch of spiritual lessons in responsibility. In this abundant universe, there's no excuse for anyone to be deprived of anything. We all have minds that can visualize anything.

The quote from Matthew (7:6) comes to mind: "Do not give what is holy to dogs and do not throw your pearls before swine...." In other words, give your light where your light is welcome. You can close your eyes and donate energy and let it be dispersed where it is accepted and needed. But what I'm hearing more is to take care of your own neighborhood, mind your own consciousness; every one of us has victim beliefs, and until we clear those, the victim/victimizer consciousness will still be in place.

This has to do with our consciousness, but there are things much bigger than this going on. This universe is vast, and there are energies coming from way beyond our solar system, which are affecting all planets everywhere. This is much bigger than just Earth. It's the whole collective movement. Those energies actually provide us a stimulus. Oftentimes people don't grow or change unless they have something acting *upon* them. Cosmic energies are providing frequencies that are acting upon our physical bodies and ourselves, allowing us new opportunities for choice and cleansing.

We're being given *light codes* that allow us to shift and change and grow at a very rapid pace. What we do with those codes will determine the result of ourselves. As a collective, humanity can change many things, but I have to tell you one of the biggest supporters we have are the animals.

The animals are getting this on a level we've never seen before. Their instinctual nature has begun to change to a more cooperative nature even amongst species that would be natural enemies.

You'll be getting more messages from the aquatic species in the sea as well. Don't be alarmed if some species leave; some species want to go home, they've been here millions of years. We need to shift our perception around them leaving from thinking that we have to keep everything here the same, while not realizing that some species are delighted to go, and it's the same with the trees. There are some species of trees that want to go Home, considering that they've been standing in one spot for hundreds of years. Many of them have been here for a tremendously long time, so you may see some tree species leaving too, so do not be alarmed.

There are many places on this planet that have gone through devastation and now have grown again, where new life has sprung up. When you see orchids and trees growing out of rocks that used to be under water, or you see rain forests thrive again after being destroyed, you can see how life renews itself here.

Q. WILL THERE EVER BE WORLD PEACE?

A. We're going to have a much larger opportunity for world peace than we've had in the past precisely because we are in a collective awakening. It is happening now. More and more people are waking up to realities they wouldn't have believed in ten years ago. Even people that we consider steeped in dogma are now starting to realize that things may not be the way they were taught.

There will be a movement toward peace, but first there will be a weeding out. There will be some who cannot handle this new paradigm that is occurring, and they will choose to leave. There is a time element here in terms of some years before you actually see things settle down on this planet where we're actually functioning in a way that we call harmonious and peaceful.

It's not going to occur overnight, although it could! There will be a new Golden Age. Certainly we're part of it, part of laying that foundation down, which is why we are here, why we are the ones that have come to raise the frequency of Earth back to its original Paradise self. In this process we do take through our bodies some of the disharmonic energies that are here. It is the reason why some people go through things that seem unusually painful.

Q. IS THERE A WAY THAT PEOPLE CAN GET INTO THE AKASHIC RECORDS AND CHANGE THE FUTURE OF WHAT'S GOING TO HAPPEN COLLECTIVELY?

A. We're all affecting the future right now with our collective choices and decisions. To presume that one person or group can deliberately go in and try to affect the collective future the way you suggest is not appropriate. If it were appropriate, Source would have done it long ago. We're all changing the future each moment by our choices, attitudes and beliefs.

See "Q. Can the Records be changed?" on page 3.

Q. HOW CAN WE BE MORE LOVING AND MORE COMPASSIONATE?

A. When you look out of your own field of vision and see things, how do you interpret them? Are you looking at things from a judgmental point of view, or are you looking at them through harmless eyes? Where are you in your heart? The truth is, love allows.

Look at your own feelings, motivations and perceptions, and be honest with yourself in terms of what conclusions you come to in your life experiences. If you find yourself separating and judging, then you know you still have not gotten the truth that we are all one movement. Everybody and everything in our outer world is a reflection of our consciousness, and it is only at the level of consciousness that true change can take place.

When you start to look at yourself and start being honest with yourself and admit that you're judging or that you're fearful of this or that, sometimes that's all that's needed to shift the energy and move on from it. The self-honesty coming to the surface is what allows for the energy to move and transform. What's underneath and what always remains, is Love.

Once you expose your own judgments to yourself, you don't have to tell them to anybody else. It's an inward process, but the effects of changing your consciousness affect the whole on the level of the Cosmic Mind.

Q. WHAT DOES 2012 HAVE TO DO WITH IT ALL?

A. The year 2012 is a peak point in terms of the influx of Light coming into the planet. You will notice time "speeding up" as we approach the end of 2012—you will see your thoughts manifesting more rapidly. Some say we are moving into the fourth or fifth dimension. Source says it is the dimension of Christ Consciousness and the return to your True Nature. Certainly the new children that are coming here are from dimensions much more advanced than ours. The fact that they can come into our planet shows you the movement we are in.

See also "Q. Is there a window of time or portal that is collapsing?" on page 145.

Q. WHAT WILL HAPPEN WITH THE FINANCIAL SITUATION IN THE WORLD IN THE NEXT COUPLE OF YEARS?

A. Money is still a difficulty until the change is sorted out. You've got to understand that this is the negative agenda's last-ditch effort, even though by Divine decree they are due to go. The NA has had control of this planet, and they are still trying to interfere with us. They are trying to control events, to change things, so that they don't have to go. It is not going to work. You will see fluctuations in commodities until our new system is put in place.

It is important to grow your own food and have a good water source as the NA is trying to control our food and water supplies. When you talk about storing food, the preference is to grow and have your own organic food supply. Getting a supply of organic seeds is recommended. Include as many medicinal herbs as you can. This is a good thing to do regardless of the NA because self sufficiency is always a good idea.

Many communities are forming now that are becoming self-sovereign—they are creating their own money system, establishing cooperative farming, becoming cooperative with all participants, *etc*. It is a time of growing up and relinquishing our co-dependence on governmental agencies that do not have our best interests at heart. The collapses that are occurring now are allowing us to make different choices and break free of these separatist and controlling systems.

Q. WHAT ABOUT MONEY IN BANK ACCOUNTS?

A. You will not be able to rely on banks or your investments as you have in the past. You will see an inevitable collapse of all systems that are based on corruption.

If we could focus on our true selves coming towards us rather than on the destructive aspects of these Earth changes, we would get through this and see many things differently. Remember what the goal is. The goal is a new Earth, and it is going to change to a new position in the solar system. We've got to keep it in perspective.

Yes, you may lose people you care about; you may see people and species leave, but by aligning ourselves with our true selves, and by keeping our auras balanced, our changing biologies will cause miracles. The more you align yourself, the more you *become* the change, the more you become an automatic field of protection for others.

Get in contact telepathically with the crystal network inside your own bodies and realize that your thoughts and your desires will be able to affect people you care about, people you love. You won't be able to change somebody's soul destiny if in fact they are one of the people that are going to go, but where you are allowed to protect, you will.

It also needs to be said that catastrophes come from the imbalances within us—specifically of our own internal masculine and feminine energies. The Earth is like any other body in that it operates to keep itself in balance however it can. Earthquakes, volcanoes and storms are her way of cleansing and restoring balance to herself. Because we are in a time of cleansing, it is important to admit that we all have had a shadow side to us. If we continue to suppress this part of us or deny it exists, it gets projected "out" and causes imbalance in the mass consciousness.

It is not God that causes Earth or climatic changes—it is the imbalances within each of us that contribute to the whole. If we can learn to inquire into ourselves and see where we are still holding judgment or un-forgiveness, and release and let the in-dwelling God Source within us guide us, we can relieve much of the "pressure" going on within and around the Earth at this time.

Suffering has never been in God's plan—it is something we cause by our misperceptions. Many times in these sessions Source has advised us to "take our world back"—not through violence, but through choosing to make this world the Paradise all worlds are meant to be.

Paradise can only come about by cooperative motives where resources are shared and greed and selfish fears are replaced with love, kindness and sharing. Each one of us must look and see where our own motives are self-seeking and choose differently. If we could all do this, there would be no need or requirement for cataclysms to occur because all would be in balance.

When you align yourself with your true self, your perceptions are going to change. As your perception changes, you will see everything that is happening in a different way. You won't be aligned with sorrow. You will be aligned with joy. As I am telling you this, your auras are already expanding!

It is important to note that there are beings coming to this planet in increasing numbers to aid us. Some are the new children that have been arriving and are still arriving, some of them are *us*, and others have been watching and waiting for the permission to come, which they now have.

Q. IS THERE A SAFE PLACE IN THE BIGGER PICTURE?

A. Your safety lies with your own relationship to your own in-dwelling God Source, or "your True self that is coming towards you," which is one and the same. Consider that your choices towards harmony and cooperation make *you* a safe place! In addition, advice has already been given to stay away from bodies of water that would be susceptible to tsunamis or flooding, as well as volcanic activity. Again, it has been advised to grow your own food and have a way to purify water. These things are wholesome things to be doing regardless of this Time of Change.

Q. WHAT HAPPENS TO THE PARTS OF THE EARTH THAT DO NOT ASCEND?

A. There is an aspect of Earth that is ascending and going to a higher frequency. Certain parts of her may "fall off" in this process, much like a snake shedding its skin. Those parts will not be ascending, but will disintegrate, much like a body would in the death process.

Q. WHAT IS THE WORLD TODAY TRYING TO TEACH HUMANS?

A. We are in a time period designed to expose the Truth on many levels and in many areas. We will all be waking up to the fraud in our banking systems, the deceit of religious dogmas, the ongoing suppression of our freedoms, to name a few. People will be shown what they believe, and what they have believed. The beliefs we have based our lives on and the systems we have relied on will show themselves to be on weak foundations. It is time to create a new way of living and to restore our basic human rights. Cooperation is the new paradigm.

Q. REGARDING NEGATIVE INTERFERENCE, ARE WE PULLING IT IN AS PART OF US?

A. If you haven't cleared your own negative perceptions, you will bring in negative interference depending on where you are at the moment in your consciousness. But remember that the majority of people have positive as well as negative perceptions. Get yourself a notebook and a pen and start to ask yourself what you think, feel and believe about the world, yourself, others, the situations in your life, *etc.*

Who have you not forgiven? It is time now to inquire into ourselves in a deeper way—to know ourselves—shadow and light. Once you take a look at your true feelings and beliefs, you can change any of it into new, more positive and loving beliefs. The time is now. We are all being blessed with more help to cleanse ourselves than ever before. Say yes!

**Indigo
Crystal
and
Rainbow
Children**

Chapter 12

Indigo, Crystal & Rainbow Children

Q. Who are the Indigo children?

A. The Indigo children are a collective of "children souls" who are coming from an Emerald Green and Golden line group of souls. They come from a particular sound harmonic level that is very pure and loving in its essence and very close to Source. The term "very close to Source" implies not a place, but an octave of light and sound. They also carry a lot of blue light and wisdom directing us towards a higher communication with our Creator. The term Indigo is akin to indigo blue in their descent to Earth, but is not the line of origin from which they come. When I approach them in spirit they all start giggling and laughing, as they are the energy of pure love, joy, playfulness and creativity guiding us toward boundless self-expression. They are here to catalyze us and challenge us to go beyond our preconceived ideas of what we believe is possible. They come from a realm that we would perceive as "Heaven" in the sense that they are the joy and delight of the Creator. This collective of children souls are not appearing as adult souls. They are appearing as a group of small, pure children souls who have agreed to come here to help lift humanity into the next Golden Age.

Q. How long have the Indigo Children been coming here?

A. At least for the last 50 to 100 years. Many of the old "geniuses" we know were Indigo children. We have been getting an influx of Indigos for some years now. They have been coming in to accelerate the evolution of our planet. The older ones going back farther in history were coming in a few at a time, but today, they are coming in huge groups especially over the last 25 to 50 years.

Q. WHY DO THESE CHILDREN COME? WHO SENT THEM?

A. Many volunteer to come to a particular planet for a particular mission.

Q. DO THE INDIGO, CRYSTAL AND RAINBOW CHILDREN ALL COME FROM DIFFERENT PLACES?

A. Yes. Indigos come from a plane in spirit, or harmonic, that is very close to Source, as mentioned previously. This harmonic is very pure, and very innocent, although containing much knowledge and wisdom. The Indigos are very sweet in their pureness and spirit. The Crystal children are at a completely different harmonic frequency than the Indigos. Think in terms of sound tones, where each soul carries a unique sound tone within them. The Crystals carry a more advanced harmonic than the Indigos in the sense they have more harmonics turned on, which allows them to have greater gifts of creativity, especially in music, sports and invention in a physical biology. They would not have been able to come here without the Indigo children coming first to set the foundation for them and doing the hard work to prepare the way for the Crystal children to come. I am still not seeing planets as origins for these children. Both types of children come from planes in spirit, although each type is from an entirely different harmonic plane.

The Rainbow children come from a place far outside of our galaxy. They don't belong to our solar system at all. There aren't a lot of them here, only very few. They're very much like little avatars. They hold a predominance of blue or Christlike energy, and they are very advanced in terms of their own personal mastery. You would most likely be in awe of them if you were to meet one. They elicit a feeling of reverence from you. We can call them the "holy people" or the "holy children." They are here predominantly to anchor peace into this planet and to help the Earth ascend into the collection of planets that function under the Christ principle. They're trying to help Earth join these other systems where the Christ principles of communication with all life, sharing and functioning goes on. There aren't very many Rainbow children here yet because our consciousness has to rise in order to hold their frequency here.

Q. WHAT IS THE DIFFERENCE BETWEEN INDIGO, CRYSTAL AND RAINBOW CHILDREN?

A. Crystal children are a more advanced form of Indigo soul. You would classify these children as more "mature" souls than Indigos. They are at a different level of advancement or different harmonic tone in their biological and energetic systems. They also feel denser than Indigos in the sense that they would have had many other biological lives in other dimensional places. Indigos feel more "pure spirit" than Crystals do. Crystals are carrying higher level coding than Indigos because their range of experience is much greater within the universe. The Indigos are from a pure, sweet, innocent vibration close to Source, almost angelic but not quite. The Crystals' higher coding gives them greater intelligence, greater knowledge and greater creative capabilities than the Indigos. You can say that the Crystal children are Indigos who are more advanced as souls. If I could use ages just for examples' sake—Crystals would be 7- to 10-year olds where Indigos would be babies. It's just a comparison, not an actuality. The Crystals carry the emerald green in their biology but also pink and blue colors.

They look even deeper into you than do the Indigos. They are here to show us that we have grown spiritually as a species whether we realize it or not. Many of us that are here are Indigos that have laid down the first energetic "grid" or foundation for the actualization of love and peace. The Crystals show us that the work the Indigos have done has succeeded. The Crystals have come here as an advancement of this foundation. Their purpose isn't mainly peace but higher intelligence, higher creativity, more advanced gifts and changes in the brain structure of humans.

There are only a few Rainbow children here. They come from an entirely different race altogether, from beyond our solar system. You would call Rainbow children true extraterrestrials in the sense that I don't see them as souls or in spirit form as I did the Indigos or the Crystals. Rather, they have come from an advanced solar system beyond our galaxy. Many carry a predominance of golden and blue light and a golden frequency within. They are here to raise this planet and all its inhabitants into a much higher frequency as a whole and into a higher planetary system. There are only a few of them on the Earth now because this is still a work in progress. More will come in as the Earth and its inhabitants integrate and incorporate this new energy. Their goal is to help Earth join in the frequency of other planetary systems that are more evolved and that function as peace-keeping planets. These Rainbow children are called "children" but they are not children in their essence. These are very advanced souls, very mature, and very Christlike. They are peace in embodiment. Indigos, in contrast, carry a very innocent and gentle peace. Rainbows carry a very mature peace, an advanced, wise peace. There is no messing around with Rainbows' consciousness. They are unity consciousness. All of their creations come from this place of reverence. Their purpose in this dimension is to build higher and higher harmonic frequencies of light into everything they do. Keep in mind that there are always higher and higher levels to achieve in spirit, in Source. They are interested in having Earth join them as a planet that carries the golden light harmonic so that its advancement and ascension can finally can be achieved. Earth has been thwarted in its efforts many times over in its attempt to ascend to higher levels. The difference now is that there are huge collectives of beings who have finally been given permission to help Earth in its ascension process. The Rainbow children look like candles lit in the universe, pillars of light carrying an incredibly powerful range of golden particles and harmonic frequencies.

The most common denominator in all these types of children is that 90% of them are very loving. Many of them are no-nonsense children. They get it, and they want to know why we are not treating each other well, why we don't cooperate with one another, why we don't work in harmony with the Earth. They already understand Love on levels that we have yet to arrive at. They are here to help us rise up into this higher way of living, loving and communicating.

Q. WHAT ARE THE MOST RELIABLE INDICATORS THAT A CHILD IS ONE OF THESE TYPES?

A. You can recognize Indigos by their unusual sensitivity and love. They are pure and sweet in their disposition, generous and highly sensitive to the feelings of others. To watch anything abusive or painful injures them tremendously. They are extremely psychic, highly intuitive and very loving to animals and to all creation. They are the ones who promote peace and think of love above all. They are of service to others as healers and counselors. They carry violet-blue and white in their auras. They may have difficulty staying grounded or tolerating artificial environments. They love the outdoors, natural things, animals, nature, and water, and they are in tune with the elementals. They always do better learning through visual or tactile experiences. They have an incredible tolerance for and patience with others. They'll smile sweetly even if they are in pain.

Crystal children, on the other hand, display the same qualities as the Indigos, but with advanced creative abilities in music, singing, or athletics. Many have memories of past lives. Crystals are characterized by their huge, round eyes.

Rainbow children are very rare and can be recognized by their peaceful, awe-inspiring presence. They emanate peace, and those who have been in their presence call them "holy." They are very direct in their communication, highly loving and compassionate, and they provide highly intelligent solutions to problems. They have ideas and higher ways of developing civilization and culture. They inspire reverence for all life everywhere. With Rainbows, it isn't what they say, it's what they emanate.

Q. HAVE THESE SOULS EVER BEEN TO EARTH BEFORE?

A. Yes, they have been to Earth before in many ancient time periods including the times of Atlantis and ancient Egypt and even before that. I have to be clear: They come and go in the sense that they wouldn't spend thousands of lifetimes here. They seem to come in, leave, and come in again and leave for specific reasons. They wouldn't be like "normal" souls that often come in and out of the Earth plane, for example. That is not to say that these children have never had "normal" lifetimes here, just not as many as would another type of soul.

Q. WHY DO THESE CHILDREN HAVE SUCH ADVANCED ABILITIES?

A. Predominantly because of the harmonics they carry from where they come from. You'd have to look at who they are as souls, the frequency of the plane of existence that they come from, and how long they've been around. The Indigo, Crystal and Rainbow children are all from different frequency bands, or harmonic levels. They have in their systems certain harmonic frequencies that are very alive, so their brains might work differently because of the harmonics they carry. Each type of child would be carrying a different combination of those, which is why one would have certain abilities, and the others wouldn't have. This allows them to express greater creative abilities.

Q. DO THESE CHILDREN HAVE PERSONAL KARMA?

A. Some do, depending on what they've done in their own particular soul journey, whether on Earth or somewhere else. Some have a certain amount of their own personal karma to work through, just as any individual soul would.

Q. ARE THERE OTHER TYPES OF ADVANCED CHILDREN COMING?

A. Yes, the Golden Ones have yet to come. These children are actually made of golden light, and they are a direct aspect of Source. These "children" seem to have halos around their heads. Not the type of halo that looks like a disc above their heads, but more like arcs around their heads. We will not see them coming here however for another 10 to 20 years. They are very masterful souls.

Q. HOW SHOULD THESE CHILDREN BE TREATED DIFFERENTLY?

A. All children should be treated equally in the sense that they all deserve to be treated with reverence for their innate creativity and intelligence and their valuable contribution to the world.

All children deserve to be treated the best way we know how. They all need love and nurturing guidance, freedom of thought, and freedom of creativity. They need to be valued for their contribution to their larger world family. All children should be fed properly, get plenty of sunlight, be out in nature, learn how to tend a garden, care for animals, and sing to the elderly. Artificial lighting should be banned, as well as foods that do not nourish or nurture.

Q. HOW CAN WE BEST HELP THESE CHILDREN CARRY OUT THEIR MISSION HERE ON EARTH?

A. We can assist them by being willing to learn from them. They challenge us to change things in our world that do not serve the highest good of the individual or the whole. They are asking us to change laws, education, and nutrition and to establish more opportunities for creative expression. They are asking us to demolish outmoded ways of thinking that limit the possibilities of individuals. They can inspire us to make changes in our world that will take us all to a much higher level of advancement. We can assist them by listening to them, paying attention to their needs in education, nutrition, and relating to our world and by making the necessary changes where they are indicated.

Q. WHY DO SOME OF THESE CHILDREN SEEM TO BE DESTRUCTIVE?

A. Some of these advanced children have a tremendous difficulty biologically integrating into the frequency of this dimension. These children are ultra-sensitives. Because they are so sensitive, exposing them to atmosphere pollution, harsh sounds, processed foods and unnatural lighting is like electrocuting them. These things weaken their immune system and dumb them down. Think of a highly tuned energy field coming down into a polluted environment by comparison. Many of these children's nervous systems have a very hard time adjusting to the harsh reality of Earth. Keep in mind how important these children are to our future. They will be the ones who will come up with advanced inventions, ways to purify water, to use energy wisely, to clean up atmospheres, to advance in science and spirituality. These are the children who are trying to take Earth to an entirely new level of functioning.

Some of the ones who have destructive tendencies may be undoing some of the collective karma of the Earth that it has inherited throughout it's history, or they may have been here in times when genius was used for destructive purposes. Indications of this would be misuses of power, the misuse of technology, and self-serving agendas that result in the destruction of the human race *etc*. Some of these children have agreed to process some of this history through their bodies in order to help Earth and its inhabitants with this unique opportunity for growth that we have now, and they may be working through their own personal karma in those time periods as well. If we could understand this, we could help them much more efficiently.

Q. ARE AUTISTIC CHILDREN INDIGO, CRYSTAL OR RAINBOW?

A. No, autistic children are souls who also carry predominantly blue energy in there auric fields, but whose forte is communication. This communication is predominantly telepathic or nonverbal. They are here to teach us to use telepathy more than words. In order for them to accomplish this, many have had to subject themselves to having their "normal" modes of communication thwarted, which forces us to stimulate communication with them nonverbally. Without us knowing, they have been teaching us how to communicate and understand using other methods. Examples of this would be by stimulating the telepathic and feeling centers in the body as well as other forms of communication that do not involve speech or words, like sign language.

The souls who take on autism are from an entirely different frequency than the Indigo, Crystal or Rainbow children. They are unique as telepathic beings, and they have agreed to come here to teach us how to have a more intimate form of communication with life in general and in so doing, encourage us to revere life on every level. On a soul level, they come from a star system beyond the Pleiades, but still in our galaxy. You would call them Beings of Light if you were to go to where they are, however they are still very much in the learning process as souls themselves. Many of them carry Venusian energy within them also and have lived many lives in other dimensional spaces. Many have also spent time on Sirius, the Pleiades, and Arcturus.

Q. HOW CAN WE BEST HELP THESE AUTISTIC CHILDREN?

A. We can best help these children by first understanding their mission by engaging in our practice of telepathic communication with them. This would also include other forms of communication that do not involve words such as touching, deep feeling and expressing ourselves through our hearts and our minds as opposed to talking. These children also need the purest forms of food, water, art, harmonious music, and tactile forms of expression such as painting, pottery, and building things. These children usually have very high intelligence, even though they may not communicate in a normal way. It would help to understand this and appreciate whom we're dealing with. Some of these children will respond to some detox programs or would benefit from finding out about foods or substances to which they would be highly sensitive.

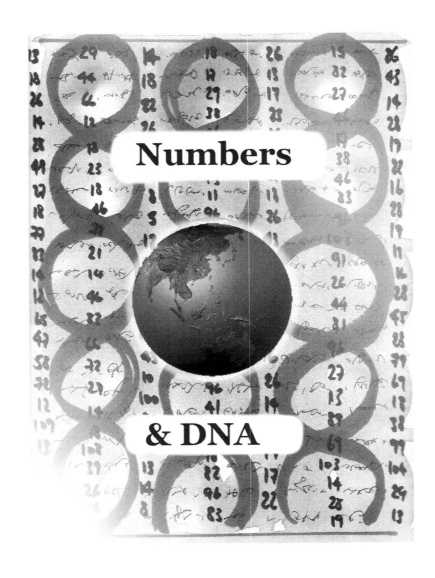

Numbers

& DNA

Chapter 13

Numbers & DNA Strands

Participant: Like most people, I'm fascinated with this whole 11:11 thing. I was born on an 11, and lived in house number 22, so the 11's have been in my life. My question however, revolves around 12's, because I feel that the 12 is more significant. Remember the 12 apostles and the number 144 in the Bible? The twelve seems to me to be a higher frequency number. It was the 12 apostles plus Jesus, who made 13. Now in this group there are 12 people plus you, which makes 13.

Q. CAN YOU GIVE US SOME IDEA IN TERMS OF NUMEROLOGY OF THE IMPORTANCE OF THE NUMBER 12 AND WHAT IT MEANS TO US, IF ANYTHING?

A. Good question! The number 12 has to do with the human being who's here on this planet right now. The *template* that the human biology is fashioned after is a base-12 system. It can achieve up to 12 dimensions of awareness, but it's limited. It is limited in that it has been that way for a long time. It's been a base-12 coding, and people like Jesus came in to introduce a higher potential to the planet.

Jesus would be considered the "13," which is a *transformational* number—a rebirth "out of an old pattern into a new pattern," but the new pattern isn't set yet. Thirteens are like a pivotal energy, offering an opportunity or shift out of a 12-based template into a new biology. The new codes have been put into place for a shift in our Earth grids, allowing the potential to unfold. It's one reason why avatars come here—to bring a new opportunity into the grids, which make it available to all the life forms on the planet. That potential is not *actualized* inside of us at this point.

Some years back I was invited to a weekend conference on an old Native American sacred site in the woods near Waterloo in Iowa. It was

Mother Mary who called this gathering together. One of the participants was an elderly man who was a Melchizedek priest. He was there
to initiate those who felt so inclined into what he called the "13:13
Doorway."

The odd thing about this gathering was who attended—there were
Aboriginal leaders from Australia, and Native American elders who
brought sacred artifacts that had never been off the reservation. There
were the rest of us—regular men and women, who were guided there. I
was personally escorted by seven hawks along the way there and was
visited by seven deer in the woods who stopped to listen to me drum
the night I arrived. Not long after that 13:13 Doorway initiation the
gray whales came to me in a vision and asked me to do grid work in
various locations around the planet.

Q. SO WE HAVE 12 STRANDS OF DNA?

A. Yes, but at this moment in time most humans have only three strands
"switched on" or working. Humans have however, a 12-strand DNA potential.
Source is helping by sending new beings and children to us that are coming in
with between four and six strands active. They're carrying frequencies that
help raise everything and everyone collectively. More and more advanced
children are coming in, and these souls are *volunteering* to come here now.
Many know these children as Indigo, Crystal and Rainbow children.

Some Indigo adults have their fourth to fifth strands active. Most humans,
in terms of actualizing those 12 strands, are not switched on to those higher
levels. The highest that has been achieved here is five to six strands turned on.
Some humans have achieved eight strands active, but they are very rare.

The special children coming in are more and more connected and
switched on in ways that we have not been. If you want to speak of the hundredth monkey, these little souls coming in are carrying these higher energies
and collectively helping to raise all of us up.

Q. MY DAUGHTER IS A PRE-K AND KINDERGARTEN TEACHER. SHE SAID IT'S PHENOMENAL THE KIDS SHE'S GETTING NOW.

A. I see it in my granddaughter as well. We need to make sure these children are kept as pure and gifted as they are. Changes in education and lifestyle are needed to do this. They need to be treated from a holistic frame of reference and kept off of drugs that dumb them down. Vaccines pollute their systems and compromise their immune systems. We need to take care of who they are and what they are offering us and this world.

Q. THERE IS MUCH DISCUSSION ON HOW DIFFERENT THESE CHILDREN ARE AND HOW THEY LEARN. CHANGE IS NEEDED IN THE SCHOOL SYSTEMS BECAUSE THEY DO NOT LEARN THE SAME WAY THAT OTHERS LEARN. THEY SAID IT'LL HAPPEN THROUGH YOUNGER TEACHERS WHO ARE MORE ATTUNED TO THESE CHILDREN. ANY COMMENTS?

A. The hands that receive these children into the world are just as important as what happens to them after.

Participant: When my grandchild was in first grade, the teacher called on each one of the kids to talk to them before parent-teacher night. She asked him how he felt about school and what he was learning. He's a very shy kid who doesn't talk very much. He sat there for a second and looked at her and said, "I already know everything you're teaching me."

Q. THE MINUTE YOU STARTED TALKING ABOUT NUMBERS, I WONDERED IF THERE IS A NEW MATH COMING THAT'S BEYOND DIGITAL. MY SENSE IS THAT DIGITAL IS GOING TO BE SUBORDINATE TO THE NEW MATH. IS THE FIBONACCI SEQUENCE GOING TO CHANGE?

A. Yes, there will be a new math, but not for some years yet. May I address the Fibonacci spiral? You all need to understand this: the Fibonacci spiral is a death spiral; it is a *finite* life spiral. Yes, I know nature has been modeled after it; yes, I know you can see it in all the sacred geometry, but it is a death spiral. It loops around again and again in on itself. The fact that all things here die proves to you that the Fibonacci mathematical sequence is programmed to death. It's not programmed to eternal life.

When our biology evolves, we will be under a new eternal life spiral. It would be incredibly wonderful if we could switch into its crystalline structure.

To answer your question, it's not being answered in terms of math, but in terms of a crystalline structure. The Fibonacci spiral creates its own type of crystalline patterns based on its geometry. You know there's crystal in all of your cells, crystals in your blood—all of those are fashioned according to the Fibonacci spiral. When I speak of a new biology, you will see change in your blood crystals and change in the crystals in your cells as well.

But it has so much to do with your own inner purification. It isn't only about your perceptions; it is also about what you do with your body. If you want your biology to shift and your blood crystals to shift, it is a divine purification process. It's what the old *inner* alchemist and the true mystics did. As you bring more love into your system, your biology and blood crystals change. It is part of what Jesus was here to do—he actually brought a higher frequency of biology and blood crystals. He once said to me, "My blood is the scent of red roses."

Q. DID JESUS EVER HAVE CHILDREN?

A. Yes he did. Part of his mission was to bring in the new blood crystals for all of humanity.

Q. HAS IT SPREAD TO ALL OF HUMANITY?

A. Yes and No. The gene code for the new blood crystals is now inherent in all races on the planet, but it has not yet become *actualized* in most people. It is up to each individual to purify his or her own consciousness for it to be actualized biologically.

Extraterrestrials

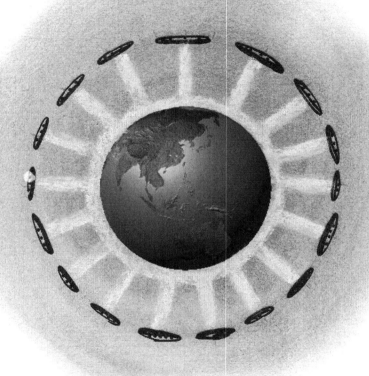

Chapter 14

Extraterrestrials

Q. WILL WE BE SEEING MORE ETs? WILL THERE BE FULL DISCLOSURE?

A. You're going to hear President Obama joke about it. I actually see him giving some campaign speech and somebody in the audience asks the question about full disclosure. He'll joke about it. He won't actually come right out and admit it, but in his joking you will know that he knows.

The problem with disclosure is that a lot of those "ships" are "ours." The government is avoiding disclosure because they don't want to have to answer all of those questions about which ships are ours and which are ET ships. Where did we get the technology? Has the government known about and supported abductions of our people in exchange for ET technology? Full disclosure would raise more questions from the public than the government cares to answer.

Think in terms of politics—the heat is already building politically with all this corruption on so many levels coming out. ET disclosure would be another instance where we would find out that we've been lied to. However, the U.S. Government has been making our own ships for years.

Q. SPACESHIPS?

A. Yes, spaceships. They are not *all* ours, but a good portion of them is. If I wanted to get into the negative ET interference, it is enough to reveal that they have been here (on Earth) all along. In other words I'm not getting negative ETs coming from a faraway place; I'm getting negative ETs that are living in our dimensional spaces right here, right now. You also have benevolent ETs here as well, and many more have now been given permission to come here and help us through this time of change.

Q. ARE YOU SAYING THE MEN IN BLACK ARE REAL?

A. Yes, they're real. Please refer to the Appendix page 180, for a description from Wikipedia – a clear example of their being part of the modern culture.

Q. SO WHEN YOU SAY NEGATIVE ETs ARE HERE IN OUR WORLD, OR CLOSE DIMENSIONAL SPACES, MY UNDERSTANDING HAS BEEN THAT THERE ARE THOUSANDS OF ETs ACTUALLY HERE ON EARTH WORKING RIGHT ALONGSIDE OF US.

A. That's true.

Q. THE BENEVOLENT ONES ARE "OUT THERE," BUT THE MORE NEGATIVE ONES ARE HERE?

A. The truth is the higher level ETs have been abiding by a Divine Decree. They have not been allowed to come closer to us until recently. They've been allowed to beam certain frequencies to us at different times. They're doing what they can as they are allowed. I do not see them *here* the way I see the negative ETs in terms of numbers. But then again, many of us are benevolent ETs who have been here many times and are here now.

Many negative ETs reside on dimensional overtones that are close to ours. That is where I see the word *sub*, "in the earth," but I also see them at very close overtones hovering in dimensional sections "above" Earth.

These negative ETs are in arrangements with government forces, and that's another reason why the governments don't want disclosure. How are they going to explain that they gave them permission to experiment on us? You'll see them laugh about it and joke about it to the public to try to make us seem foolish for believing in UFOs and ETs.

Q. AT SOME POINT DOESN'T ALL THAT HAVE TO COME OUT?

A. There are some governments that are exposing the truth about it, but those are governments that are not in arrangement with those ETs. Some of you may have seen the Canadian, Mexican and Peruvian governments come out and talk about it. It's no secret in Peru—there are signs all over. But in terms of the U.S. government exposing itself, I don't see it happening anytime soon.

It's going to become less and less important if the government actually comes out and admits it, because the people will be getting the truth through other sources. Indeed, inside each one of us, the truth is being known more and more. The people are not going to need the government to come out and reveal the truth, they will already know it.

(See also "Q. Did extraterrestrials create us in their perception, or are we creating them in our perception?" on page 146.)

Prosperity

Chapter 15

Prosperity

In this section we asked Source about money and prosperity. Source answers these questions at the level they are being asked, but ultimately lets us know that manifesting is a game. It's like children playing until they know, understand and trust that God's will for them is perfect happiness and that their will for everyone is the same as God's.

At this point the difference between perceiving a lack that needs to be "manifested" is replaced with the knowing that everything has already been received and that, ultimately, we are sustained by God's Love.

We all run certain unconscious programs about money, some more convoluted than others. We've been brought up to define our self-value by it. What kind of patterns might we all have that keep our prosperity from us?

While saying the prayer, I saw a beam of light blue light come down, and the first thing Source said is that prosperity has to do with communication to and from Source. What we're all missing is the awareness of our direct communication to and from Source.

Q. WHAT IS SOURCE'S DEFINITION OF PROSPERITY?

A. Everything that's ever been created in the universe—creation itself—is the ultimate prosperity. Source describes creation as "wonderment." We don't perceive the wonderment of "everything that is" in a big enough way. "Prosperity" is also direct communication with all life. In other words, if we were in an aware state of prosperity, we would be able to communicate with people, birds, animals, trees and plant life—all life everywhere. This communication is prosperity.

It is the awareness that everything is conscious and can be communicated with regardless of its separate or individual appearance. The point Source is making is that we're all connected to everything, and if we could truly feel that, or know it as an ongoing awareness, we'd always be in a state of abundance/prosperity because we'd be in a *conscious flow* with life.

The prosperity that Source is talking about isn't about money *per se*, except to the extent that money is included in the "All That Is." Source is explaining that because life never ends and everything is eternal, there is nothing but prosperity. Think of it—as I'm seeing visions of things expanding, expanding and expanding, the idea of lack is so false, so illusory to this realization. There's no such thing as lack. It doesn't exist. The idea of lack is the first misperception or miscommunication that we have. That we believe in lack at all, or perceive lack as a reality shows us how distorted our minds have become.

Now, I just saw the color red. This color has presented itself on more than one occasion in these groups—so much so that we really need to pay attention to it. It may be the color for abundance at this physical level of reality. It may be the grounding frequency. Even though we look and see green grass, green trees and green plant life, it seems at the level of a physical spectrum, things need the red spectrum to materialize, or "ground."

The mineral and elemental kingdoms—the kingdom of nature—have a lot to do with what gets "produced" here. There's actually a lot of red in that spectrum in terms of a grounding energy or an elemental influence that contributes to prosperity or the abundance of life forms at this level. As we have been shown red has to do with materializing forms at the 3-D physical level.

The color frequencies associated with each chakra begin to take on new meaning when we realize that, not only are colors information, but each appears to be connected to a different aspect of life.

Source is also telling me that our chakras (our internal vortices) aren't clear. I'm feeling breath and hearing tones go through them. If our chakras were really clear, and our "cones" were working properly (they're like megaphones)—they would allow us to be in direct communication with the worlds around and within us.

When they're not functioning correctly—and there could be many reasons why they aren't—we're not able to receive the information that's within and around us. Each chakra is tuned to communicate with the different worlds that are within and around us.

When they're vibrating correctly, they're like ears. (Our actual "ears" are also chakras) Like ears, you hear tones through the chakras similar to tuning forks. They each vibrate at different frequency levels and are designed to attune us or connect us to the different frequency levels or bands of the various kingdoms around and within us. It's not limited to our three-dimensional world but incorporates many dimensional levels or realities within it.

Source has not mentioned "money" at all yet, but we can see why understanding the prosperity that is everywhere is a prerequisite to understanding the illusion of lack in any form.

Q. WHY DO WE STRUGGLE?

A. Struggle is a consequence of our belief in death. It goes back to the idea that we're sinners, that we're guilty, that we have that original Guilt/Sin. If we believe that about ourselves, and obviously that's demonstrated and taught here on Earth, then lack is a natural consequence of that belief system.

In other words, if you believe in guilt, then you have to believe in punishment. If you believe in punishment, you will believe you're going to be judged. If you believe in judgment, you're going to judge others. If you judge others, you're going to feel guilty. If you feel guilty, you're going to punish yourself, and on and on it goes. You punish yourself through lack, illnesses, death and all sorts of things being taken from you, and not just things being taken from you, but also by not allowing yourself to have or receive certain things. You will punish yourself in myriads of ways.

It must be said that it is not Source that punishes—it is our own belief in sin and guilt. This belief is all encompassing in our world and is a core belief structure—our entire judicial system is based on it. It's a snowball effect. If everybody believes in death, then everybody creates death for themselves.

I am reminded of a time when I studied rebirthing. The people who created rebirthing (Sondra Ray and Leonard Orr) call themselves "Immortalists." They believe that we were never supposed to die. They said it well when they would say, "All death is suicide." Source is reinforcing that, saying that's actually true, and Source does not demand death of us.

If death were natural in Source, what would be the point of Ascension? It is easy to see how these beliefs create lack and all the rest of it, being the direct opposite of the Life Principle, which is multiplication. Source is saying that if you really knew your relationship with it, you would be in a state of bliss, ecstasy and abundance, because that's what Source is. Source considers its creation to be ecstasy.

If we really understood our relationship with all things, which *is* Source, a) we would never have a harmful thought toward anybody, and b) we would be in joy always, which would naturally create abundance and prosperity for us. The flow of prosperity would naturally be ever present.

Q. A LOT OF PEOPLE WILL SAY THAT IT'S VERY EASY TO MANIFEST PROSPERITY, YET FOR A LOT OF PEOPLE, IT'S ACTUALLY VERY DIFFICULT TO MANIFEST PROSPERITY. WHY IS THAT?

A. People feel guilty about being prosperous due to what we have already explained. If you feel that there's going to be a consequence to something you manifest, you won't allow yourself to have it. And if you do, you will destroy it for yourself eventually in some way. Look at the people who have fame or millions of dollars—you will often hear how they destroy themselves with drugs or alcohol, or they become so egotistical that they lose favor with others.

Every illness is really self-punishment in some way. When illness manifests in you, it is a part of you that doesn't believe in your own innocence—that you're loved by God. Beneath all suffering and lack is the unhealed core belief in guilt and punishment. That's the problem. When people say they want something (it doesn't have to only be money—it could be a relationship, a new car, *etc.*), and if they have a subconscious equation that associates the object of their desire with a negative consequence of some type, they will not allow their desire to manifest. They may simply believe it is impossible for them to have that object, or that the consequences of having it outweigh its benefits.

The exception to this is when your soul contract has arranged "safe-guards" for you to not be waylaid or distracted by certain things or ways of life that would be unproductive for what you are trying to accomplish in this life.

Sometimes people know, for example, that if they were to suddenly manifest things they desire, they'd leave people, places or existing relation-ships in their lives so they worry about the effect of that on others. There are many subconscious beliefs about prosperity within each one of us that deserves our honest examination. Journaling about your beliefs is a great exercise.

Q. IS THERE ANY WAY TO GET RID OF GUILT?

A. Source says, "To release guilt, you first have to stop believing in it and then release the fear that is attached to it." Let's talk about fear because Source is saying that along with the belief in guilt is the fear of eternal dam-nation. Only Source can prove to you that you're loved, forgiven and inno-cent. It can't be fixed from your own fear-based belief structure. You have to go higher to do it. You have to go to the "place" or "level" where there is no guilt—and that is to God Source Itself, which lives within all of us.

Guiltlessness will be demonstrated to you when you're ready to believe in it. It isn't that you've never made a mistake in your life—it means that Source doesn't judge mistakes. In other words, all Source looks at is the Love in Its creation.

There has to be a willingness to truly release fear. Not only is your own willingness needed, but are you really willing to give up judgment of your-self and everybody else too? Think of all those opinions that you have every time you look at someone and perceive that they're guilty of this or that?

Understanding and experiencing innocence (we are equating "inno-cence" with prosperity here) means that all belief in guilt and judgment has to go. If you are willing, innocence will be proven to be true of you, and also true of everyone else. When you get to this place of harmlessness, abundance will be natural because you will be in the flow of Divine Love.

Source says, "I'm the only one that can undo what man has made. I'm the only one that can prove it to you because I Am Truth."

Q. WHEN YOU SAY EVERYBODY NEEDS THE HELP OF SOURCE, AND YOU DEFINED PROSPERITY AS THAT DIRECT COMMUNICATION THAT'S MISSING, HOW DOES ONE PRACTICALLY ACCOMPLISH THAT?

A. It may sound simple and "etheric," but the truth is, all you really need to do is ask Source to prove to you that you're innocent, that *you*, and everybody else is innocent. You don't have to worry about how that's going to happen. You just have to be willing to have it happen. That's number one. Communication is what comes after that. It's the natural consequence of being free of the belief in guilt and punishment. When you start removing guilt and fear beliefs, you suddenly start to automatically feel at one with everything because there is no fear blocking love. Communication with Source doesn't necessarily always mean that you're going to hear Source's voice, although it certainly can. It will most likely begin as a feeling of love and unity and a shift in how you see things.

An example can be the reports of people who have had a near death experience (NDE). When they come back from them, they all say that colors look brighter, the world looks more beautiful, they're at peace, and suddenly they see everybody in a different way. Having had an experience of the Love and beauty of God, they have no more fear.

You could also begin to see the energy fields that surround everything. You could be holding something in your hand and it could start to communicate with you. It could be any level. You could receive things you've always desired. Things in your life suddenly begin to "flow" and show up for you, from a feeling or an experience to what you would call a miracle in your life. Something suddenly happens that wouldn't "normally" have happened. Source will prove it to you, to each one of you, in a way, in a language that you can recognize.

Q. SO, THE NEXT QUESTION IS: WHAT ARE THE BIGGEST BLOCKAGES TO PROSPERITY?

A. Aside from what we have already mentioned before, "mind control" by interfering sources is another factor. I specifically see the area behind our backs from the bottom of the spine to the shoulder blade area. Source is saying that there's a vortex between the shoulder blades where we are being bombarded with low frequencies from not so nice beings that actually have kept a type of "veil" over us that keeps us in fear and survival mode. There's a nerve or ganglion connection point between the shoulder blades that flows into other nerve centers that affect the brain. Because it affects the brain, it affects the endocrine system, which affects the hormones in our system and the types of chemicals they produce. Hormones affect your moods and feelings, and how clear or unclear you can be.

There are all kinds of ways that we're being pulsed or controlled by suggestions and beliefs that we're sinful, powerless and lowly creatures. Source is saying that the big program in our system is all about death and its many disguises. Death and survival are the two main things that the NA keeps us in fear about.

Fear of survival and God's wrath produce death chemicals in our bodies. Because we don't get past that, we stay afraid. We all need to let go of these beliefs. Let's not underestimate how deep this program is within all of humanity. It is the reason why history keeps repeating itself. It is evident that we don't understand how deep it goes. It's so deep that we actually have nerve chords that vibrate to those death beliefs that affect our brain. What is also true, however, is that we have every chemical in our brains to heal anything at all. We haven't been able to access that part of ourselves because we're in constant survival mode and fear, which creates stress hormones instead of healing hormones.

Q. HOW DO WE REPROGRAM OURSELVES?

A. Let's not use the word "reprogram" since we have all been negatively programmed for eons. Instead, let's call it our "reawakening" to our *true nature*. To help with this, we can see ourselves bathed in violet, purifying light every day, morning and evening and even throughout the day if something troubles you. It has powerful transmutation powers and is a very high frequency band. Source is also showing me a golden-white cord attached to your crown chakra (in the area of your "soft spot" on the top of your head) that leads directly up to Source.

Q. A SILVER CORD?

A. No, it's golden, not silver. Visualize this cord every day—see that it's intact and that it is connecting you to Source. The reason you are to see it from there as opposed to your heart or somewhere else, is because the crown of your head deals with your brain centers. It's the brain wiring that's affected by negative pulsing.

When you start consciously making this connection to Source every day, you will notice your thoughts and feelings changing and becoming more positive. The truth is that Source is here all the time and is within you, but there's a certain frequency it wants to actually bring into the brain.

So, the violet light and connecting the golden-white cord to Source are the two suggestions being given. Interestingly, Source is interjecting here and saying that any one of you who is surrounded by or near young children, connect their cord back too. Simply touch the top of their heads and connect their cord back in your mind. Children are being pulsed as well by the NA.

Q. WITH MANIFESTING, HOW MANY TRIES DO WE GET TO ACHIEVE A DESIRE?

A. I worked in a bookstore some years ago, and at the time I wanted to manifest a particular type of house. A woman came into the store, and we were metaphysically chatting when she said to me, "Well you know, if Source brings you a house that's 80% what you want, you better take it because you won't get another opportunity." That comment just did not feel right to me so I said to her, "That would be like believing Source isn't smart enough to give me exactly what I desire." It's also suggesting that you wouldn't have another chance, or that there's a limited amount of opportunity out there.

What I'm hearing from Source is that idea *is* absolutely ridiculous. To have only one chance would go against the "Art of Prosperity."

Some limiting beliefs around that could be: "I am not good enough to get exactly what I want. I might be good enough to get half of what I want, but not all of it."

Q. SO, HOW DO YOU HANDLE THAT? WOULD YOU SAY TO SOURCE, "YOU DIDN'T GET IT RIGHT, SOURCE," OR WOULD YOU SAY, "I APPRECIATE THAT VERY MUCH, BUT GO AGAIN"?

A. The truth is that it's the measure of your own consciousness, really. Again, you would take a look at that and say, "Am I willing to really accept this 80%? Compared to what I'm living in now, the 80% is a whole lot better, I better take it." The situation will measure your own belief systems and your own fear of what you think you can or can't have. Can there be a perfect house, for example? And if so, am I allowed to have it? Do I deserve to have it? Do I believe I *am* Love Itself?

Q. AND THEN OF COURSE, THERE COULD BE A HUGE LEARNING CURVE, WHICH SAYS, "I MANIFESTED AT 80%, SO I'M GETTING GOOD. BUT I DESIRE 100%."

A. Yes, that's right! What Source is saying is, "Do you really think I couldn't provide a perfect house for you if you desired it?"

Q. I'VE ALWAYS WANTED TO HAVE A HOUSE OF MY OWN. I HAVE A HOUSE, IT'S NOT MINE. I WAS ALWAYS TOLD THAT I WILL GET A HOUSE, BUT I'M STILL WAITING. CAN YOU ASK SOURCE ABOUT THAT?

A. In your particular case, there are a few reasons why you have not manifested your own house. There are parts of you that are not particularly happy with your life, and not particularly happy with whom you're living with. When we talk about consequences, the idea of a perfect house with that person isn't really what you want, first of all.

The other thing is that there is this part of you that feels guilty for judging this other person, the situation, and the relationship, so there are all kinds of reasons why you wouldn't really let yourself have it. If you were to suddenly have this house and you moved into it with this other person, you might still feel as trapped as you do now.

Participant: Just as you said that, I got that flash, and I knew myself, that it was I who was not allowing the new house to be.

Source is saying that if you're not manifesting what you desire, it is because of some negative association going on within you about your desire. Guilt and fear are really the biggest issues of why people don't manifest what they desire.

Just a little example from our life: We were out looking at beds today. We're having guests come soon, so we need another bed. Here were our thoughts about spending the money for the beds:

"Do we allow ourselves to get a good quality, comfortable bed, because it's a $100 more than the other bed? If we spend that money now, what about the rent and groceries?"

We were watching a part of us that was fearful about the loss we'd incur if we bought the better bed. It's a small example, but the truth is that all those decisions are examples of how well we love ourselves. We decided to get the good bed because we need a good bed and the woman coming to visit us is 77, and she's just a wonderful woman and gracious as can be, and I want her sleeping on something comfortable and worthy of her.

The lesson in this was for us to watch the fear come up and to say "yes" anyway despite the fear because the decision was one of loving ourselves and our guests. We don't know how the money is going to come yet, but that's the part where we say to the universe, "Well, it's just going to have to come. I don't know how, but it's going to come."

(Note: The money *did* come soon after!)

Q. WHAT IS SOURCE'S OPINION ABOUT MONEY?

A. Source doesn't actually have an opinion about money, but I am being shown coins thrown up in the air saying, "What a wonderful thing!" Source has no judgment of it either way, but it would prefer we use it with an air of enjoyment and not consider it our identity or a replacement for God's Love.

Money is neutral. It's part of what's been created or made here. Source didn't make it; man made it, but, Source says, "Have a ball." Source doesn't have any judgment around it. I think that's really important to realize. Source considers it a neutral entity that we created and is saying, "Why wouldn't you have fun with it just like you would with anything else?" Have it or don't have it, it's all the same to Source.

The problem we all have, is even if we were to suddenly get millions of dollars, if we haven't fixed the communication issue that we talked about earlier, we still won't be happy. We can't think of money as the answer to all our problems, or that it's the magic pill to happiness. Happiness is communication with Source. Since money is neutral, there is no judgment around it. How it's used determines whether it is a blessing or a curse.

Q. DOES SOURCE THINK WE SHOULD KEEP MONEY IN THE HUMAN RACE?

A. You would be better to keep money rather than have a system where everything is on credit, or on a microchip. Money is a medium of exchange and would work fine if people used it as a free-flowing medium of exchange without hoarding or greed. *(See "Stop hoarding" on page 34.)*

As I mentioned you will see communities coming into being that are inter-dependent within themselves and have their own monetary system. This keeps it out of government and bank control.

The NA is trying to destroy the money system in order to create a one-world system based on plastic cards and microchips, which would make it impossible to be free to use money in our own way. All usage would be tracked and controlled. This is a violation of the laws of free will and self-sovereignty.

Q. WHY IS THERE SUCH AN UNEVEN DISTRIBUTION OF WEALTH?

A. The main problem is that we don't believe we can have it, just the same as the next person. We have been so convinced of lack and we so believe it that it looks like only the people in power have the money.

Because they have the wealth, they're the ones who dictate where it goes. But the real problem, Source is saying, is that we don't accept it for ourselves. We're so programmed to believe that we can only have what we earn—that there's only certain ways to achieve money or wealth. We have such a limited perception of the flow of money that we don't allow it to come to us easily. Because we don't allow it to come to us, we don't have it to give. So, it looks like the powers in control have all the money, and they do have a lot of money, so they have no problem with it. They control where it goes, but Source says "You could have a lot too." Then you could do what you wish with it.

It is about knowing that there is a principle of infinite supply in the universe, and once you know it and believe in it, anything is possible. You don't have to be concerned with how it will come to you, just know that it will.

Remember, however, that money is not happiness. Nor is that perfect house, or relationship, *etc.* Happiness is when you are in communication with all life everywhere and you know yourself as everything, which is Love.

Q. WHY IS THE WORLD IN SUCH AN ECONOMIC RECESSION NOW?

A. There are many things shifting and changing, first of all. The answer I'm hearing is that the NA is taking advantage of the cosmic cycles we are now in. I have to distinguish the two. The first thing Source is showing me is that we are in a period of transition. It's just a cosmic fact. Now, that period of transition, if you left it alone, would actually be a pretty blissful experience if there weren't any interference. The NA is causing the recession to keep people in survival mode because they don't want their system of control interrupted.

They know we are waking up to the Truth on all levels as this cosmic cycle brings more Light onto the planet. So, instead of having you wake up, the NA would prefer to keep you scared and dependent on them. This recession is created by the NA.

On the one hand, we have an opportunity for more self-mastery, part of which is examining fears that you have and finding out what makes you too afraid to expand because of what you might lose. All kinds of security issues will be surfacing for people. Comfort zones will be challenged on many levels—whether it's finances, relationships, family, health or something else, because the interfering parties want to weaken you on all those fronts.

Mastery means that we have to get a hold of ourselves. Source says "Look: I'm giving you a feed line to me. You need me. You can't get out of your fear yourself. You need help from a higher part of yourself that's not in fear."

Q. THE NA IS TERRIFIED THEN, OF THE INDEPENDENCE WE COULD HAVE?

A. Absolutely. We wouldn't need them. For example, take something like oil; the truth is we don't need oil. We have the technology for other forms of energy and automobiles that run on other sources of energy that don't pollute our environment. It's been around for years—it's not new. Why don't they bring it out? Because the oil companies' whole existence is dependent on our consuming oil, and that's what's running the world.

The pharmaceutical companies are the same. Each of us needs to become more self-reliant and incorporate other forms of energy in our homes and healing in our lives.

Q. IN TERMS OF PROSPERITY, AND THE UNEVENNESS OF THE DISTRIBUTION OF WEALTH AND ECONOMIC DOWNTURNS, IS IT ALSO THE CASE THAT IF WE MASTER OUR ATTITUDES AROUND MONEY, PROSPERITY AND ABUNDANCE, IT WILL HELP THE WORLD?

A. Anything you heal helps the collective. You are either part of the problem or part of the solution.

It's true that if you clear your fear around money, you may not experience the lack of it, but that's not the point. The point is whether you have it or you don't have it, when you're in communication with Source and with life, money isn't your goal or your happiness. You're not dependent on material things to define yourself. The reason why people crash and burn when their money or possessions get taken from them is because their identities are attached to it. Then people feel they have nothing to live for.

We need to be reminded that our money and possessions are not our real identity. It's an interesting challenge to suddenly go through Earth changes or job loss, or whatever we may go through. Source is saying that you're not connected to real prosperity if you're so worried that you're going to lose a few dollars. There's always more money, just like there's always more of everything, really.

This idea that there are not enough resources in the world is ridiculous. It only appears that way because of the controlling of the distribution of goods.

We were looking at a chestnut tree in Ireland one day and AHONU said, "Do you see all the chestnuts on that tree? There are hundreds of chestnuts, thousands probably, on one tree!" How could you possibly say that there isn't enough? Look at the abundance on all the trees and everywhere!

Communication with Source is happiness. Not anything else.

Participant: Even as children, we're programmed so early about saving the money in the money box, because if you don't save it, you won't have it. Really think about how early that programming starts. You have to put it away for a rainy day. There's not enough to go around. As you rightly said about resources too, I remember my parents being very frugal with electricity and heat or fuel and food. As a child I was already embodying the fear that there isn't enough.

Yes, it needs to be said that when we're really in a prosperity consciousness, we wouldn't waste resources. There's a tendency to think, "Well, if I knew there was an infinite supply everywhere, who cares? Crank up the heat!" The truth is, the more conscious you become of life, the more you're interested in not wasting. That doesn't mean you conserve out of fear; it means you wouldn't waste just as you wouldn't harm.

People may think that if I tell you all that you are innocent and that there's no judgment except for what we do to ourselves, that it means you have a license to do anything you want because God's not going to judge you. Once you start to feel that communication with Source, you become more and more harmless. You don't have harmful thoughts. You don't have harmful desires. They don't enter your consciousness at all.

Q. WHY DO I ALWAYS FEEL GUILTY FOR MANIFESTING?

A. It is because you may not be manifesting anything real. Even though you manifest something, there is a sorrow around it because what you thought it was going to give you, it didn't give you. It makes you feel that you did something wrong because it didn't give you the result that you thought it would. But you didn't do anything wrong. You just didn't do anything real. What's real is to know yourself as God knows you. Then you will always be filled.

The NA tries to tell us that we need to be kept under a tight rein because we can't be responsible for ourselves, or we're not intelligent enough to be masters of our own lives. We think we need these authority figures to tell us what to do, to create rules. How many rules get created because one bad apple does something? Suddenly the whole group is penalized because one person is not acting responsibly.

When there's a storm and the stoplights go out, I've never seen an accident. I've always seen people stop when a stop light goes out—one car goes, the next car goes... we're all courteous to each other. The NA has been convincing us that we have to be tightly controlled because we don't have the intelligence to figure things out ourselves. Consider what our world would be like if we offered love to it rather than competition or guilt?

Q. WOULD YOU SAY THAT THE ART OF PROSPERITY IS ABOUT AN ATTITUDE OF MIND THAT OBVIOUSLY FLOWS FROM THE CONNECTION TO SOURCE?

A. The art of prosperity is more than just an attitude of mind—it's a way of being. It is actually *you being* prosperity. You become it, which is very different than saying, "I'm thinking differently." Thinking differently would be a natural consequence of *"being"* prosperity. *"Being"* prosperity is being in communion with all life—where you *know* that everything and everyone *is* you. There is no separation between you and anyone or anything else. You know you literally *are* all of everything and everything is you. When you truly know this, you are in communion, and communion *is* prosperity.

Q. HOW CAN WE MAKE THE EARTH MORE PROSPEROUS?

A. The Earth is already prosperous. That's not the problem. The problem is the distribution of goods. As long as we all hold lack beliefs, we all contribute to the unequal distribution of resources. The idea of lack creates lack. But when we shift that around, we create an energy, an opening.

Think of it more on a quantum level of the universe in terms of how things would manifest. The Intelligence that is Source takes our thoughts and says, "Yes," to them, whatever they are. It doesn't differentiate whether they are good thoughts or bad thoughts, it just says, "Yes." It makes more.

If we hang on to lack beliefs and guilt beliefs, that is what we create more of. Because of these beliefs, there's always more lack, death and disease. All these conditions springboard off each other, which is why they don't shift. It's only when each one of us starts to clean up our beliefs that we will see conditions "out there" shift.

You'll first start to see your own life shift, and then you will notice that you are treated and seen differently by others. You are either prosperous or you're not, well or unwell, happy or unhappy. You can't be both extremes at once, and there is no gray area. Either extreme is a choice.

Carolyn Myss has a story about a time when she had to give a lecture in Chicago during a riot. She was going down a most dangerous street, and no one touched her, even though cars were being bombed and overturned. She drove through it all untouched because she held her belief in peace and safety.

I've had experiences of my own, more than once, where I've been in dangerous situations and was unusually shielded from the danger. Changing our beliefs and choosing different thoughts automatically starts to affect our lives, and this begins to affect the whole of life for the better.

Participant: My father never locked the door to our house, the whole 50 years we lived there. He did get robbed one time; they took the TV and a few things, but one time in 50 years and he still didn't lock the door after that. Years ago, it was quite common to see the key in the front door or on a string. I thought it was the most beautiful thing. Talk about living in trust with your neighbors and your community! It would be nice to get back to that place of trust, wouldn't it?

Q. I HAVE A QUESTION ABOUT THE CONNECTION WITH SOURCE. I SHOULD PROBABLY MEDITATE MORE, BUT I FIND IT DIFFICULT. YOU'RE SAYING WE NEED TO START MORE OF A COMMUNICATION, OR A RELATIONSHIP, WITH SOURCE. IS MEDITATION THE BEST WAY TO DO THAT?

A. Not necessarily. Source said all you have to do is have the desire and the willingness. It can be your own unique prayer from your heart or you could be walking down the street to catch the bus, and say to Source, "I desire a demonstration of connection with you." Sometimes I qualify that and say, "That doesn't mean that I want to die or have a near-death experience." I am clear about that. "Not through any tragedy." I am clear about this because people can manifest tragedies by desiring a connection to Spirit, which their sub-conscious takes literally, and they may suddenly find themselves leaving the planet and reuniting with Spirit.

So you have to be very clear and specific to ask for an experience *here*, on Earth, while still in your body. You don't have to meditate, but if that's your best way to establish your relationship with Source, you will have the desire to do it. You could also have a dream or some other experience. It could really be anything. You could be sipping a cup of coffee and suddenly have a "Wow!" moment, and a light bulb goes on, or you have a revelation. It could be anywhere, anytime, doing anything, in any type of way.

Participant: I'll tell you a little story about that. My mother, who was very religious, used to tell us when we were small that a bunch of young boys were out playing football on the village green, and the next thing, God appeared to them and said, "The world is ending in 24 hours." All but one of them scattered home and told their mothers they loved them and then confessed all their "sins." One little boy kept playing football, kept dribbling the football around and God said to him, "Hey, how come you haven't run off with the rest of them?" And he said, "Well, I'm doing what makes me the very happiest. And when I'm happy, it feels like I am with you." It was a beautiful little lesson. I think it's a lesson in prosperity, too, because that was that communication that we're talking about.

Q. AS WE'RE MAKING THOSE CHANGES IN OUR CONSCIOUSNESS AND IN OUR BELIEF SYSTEMS, MUST WE COME INTO CONFLICT WITH THOSE THAT DON'T WANT THAT TO HAPPEN? OR IS THERE ANOTHER WAY?

A. You mean once your consciousness starts shifting from guilt to inno-cence, will you have conflict with others who don't want to change? You may be challenged by others. Challenges are oftentimes the way you find out if you've really shifted. The answer is that you'll actually have both things happen. Positive things will happen as well as some challenges. The challenges will get less and less.

It is true that there can be people around you that don't want to shift. There's no guarantee that changes will always go smoothly. But when you start to shift, you actually have both things turn up initially. What I find is that once you've really shifted, you'll no longer have those challenges.

When I was in metaphysics early on I wanted my mother and the people around me to know what I was doing because I was so happy that I was finding truth. I had so much opposition from my family. I had one aunt who sent me a book on entity possessions—she was sure I was possessed—a big, thick book. I actually read it and learned so much from it. I actually thanked her. It confirmed for me that I definitely was *not* possessed!

It took me about seven years through various other confrontations and challenges to get really clear and certain that how I was changing was a good thing. When I was learning the Tarot, it seemed like no matter where I moved, the Jehovah Witnesses would be knocking at my door. They had their little booklets, and they didn't know me from a hill of beans, but they'd always open the page with the Tarot cards, saying they were evil. I'd go back in the house and think, "Are they evil? Am I wrong?" It actually took me some years to work through it. That's how ingrained the fear of God was within me.

It can be a real challenge to get over the fear of "authority figures" who tell you that the changes you're making are evil. I would worry, "Do they know more than me?" It took me a long time to figure out that they didn't and that they were simply following a belief system that somebody taught them.

Thankfully, I had the desire and ability to inquire within myself—to sit down and ask myself and my in-dwelling God Presence for truth. So you do get challenged when you're shifting beliefs—it's a part of the "curing" process! I can even say too, with a relationship that I had that I actually had to get divorced in order to be myself.

That doesn't happen to everybody; some people's partners change along with them. Mine didn't, and I was left with another challenge. It became very uncomfortable for me to be living with a partner who was telling me I was nuts, and it would make my friends feel uncomfortable as well. He used to mock me and call me "The Wisdom of the Ages."

My children took it on in a positive way, and they'd say, "Well, she is, Dad!" Those challenges aren't fun, but sometimes they can be the way it plays out. In order for you to move forward, sometimes you have to let go of what's not supporting you.

I'll give another example. In the Tarot, there are certain cards that are just not fun. The Tower is a good example because it is a card of catastrophe. The point of that card is that it's only catastrophe if you've been getting promptings all along from your Spirit to change or grow and you've been ignoring them. So, it'll collapse something in your outer environment in order to cause a change. If the foundations in your life are not on a right footing, the Tower will collapse things in your life. But if you learn to take direction from your Spirit, and you move through your fears and you shift, you won't be pulling that card anymore. You'll be pulling other cards that support growth, that are easier and more positive.

Q. CAN YOU SUMMARIZE FOR US HOW TO ESTABLISH THIS COMMUNICATION WITH SOURCE?

A. Yes. Source is being really clear that all you have to do is tell Source that you want it demonstrated in your life. In other words, you allow Source to come in and do it; you don't have to figure out how it's going to happen.

Source gave us a few very simple things to do to establish this communication:

- Use your visualization to strengthen the golden-white cord from your crown to Source by picturing your line going directly to God Source.
- Bathe yourself in violet light and then ask Source to give you a demonstration of communication in a way that you can recognize and understand.

I'll tell you about the woman who scribed *A Course in Miracles* just because it makes the point. Her name was Dr. Helen Schucman, a psychiatrist and atheist. She worked with another psychiatrist named Bill Thetford and they had difficulty getting along. One day, they were walking down the hall and Bill said, "There must be a better way." As if on cue Helen replied, saying, "You're right. I'll help you find it." That's all they did. Suddenly Helen started having a series of dreams. In one dream in particular she recognized herself in a past life, which shocked her, because she was an atheist and didn't believe in those things. The dream was an ancient life, and she was in a boat which led her to a cave where there was a book. She opened the book and read the title. It was a Greek word meaning "Healing."

The series of dreams kept coming. She dreamt of a church in a particular town and she knew she had lived there in another life. She asked Bill, "Will you go with me to see if this church really exists?" They went to the town and found that the church she dreamt of was not there. She thought she must have been crazy or wrong, so she went to the town library and did some research. Sure enough, there had been a church there long ago.

Not too long after that she was sitting home alone and heard a voice say, "This is a Course in Miracles. Please take notes." Thus began a telepathic dictation. The author of the Course identified itself as Jesus, which also challenged her beliefs as an atheist. The scribing went on for seven years. She'd go to work, and come back home, pick up the scribing where she left off, and the flow was never interrupted.

One day she showed the scribing to Bill, who offered to transcribe it for her. When Jesus kept saying he was the author of the Course, Helen asked him to "Prove it." Jesus told her he would prove it and asked her what she wanted of Him. Helen loved clothes shopping and bargains. She wanted to be shown where to find the best bargains. "Go to this or that store," Jesus would tell her. She'd go off and sure enough the bargains would be there. This went on for months, and this to her was love and the proof she needed that Jesus was who he said he was. Finally after three or four months of it, Jesus said to her, "Can we stop these foolish games now?"

The point is he also told her that if someone's hungry, you don't hand them *A Course in Miracles*; you bring them food. That's the level on which they need to know they're loved. Somebody else may be ready for higher levels of awareness. Source will communicate with you and prove to you that you're loved in the best way for *you*.

Q. IN THE BIGGER PICTURE, YOU'RE CHANGING YOUR PERSONAL PERCEPTIONS AND BELIEFS. TAKE THAT FURTHER AND YOU'RE ATTEMPTING TO CHANGE SOCIETY. IS IT INEVITABLE THAT YOU WILL ENCOUNTER RESISTANCE?

A. Yes, because the fundamental error is that you're trying to change society. Source says, "If you were truly in communication with life, you wouldn't have a desire or a need to change society."

Q. WHAT ABOUT CHANGING AN EXISTING, LIMITING SYSTEM TO A MORE HARMONIOUS AND EXPANDED SYSTEM?

A. To the degree that the people you are trying to shift are invested in the system, you can expect challenges. What I have seen here tonight is that the system hasn't really changed in hundreds of years because the fundamental consciousness of the world hasn't changed. You always have those who want a system to be a certain way. Any rabble rouser to the system is not going to be welcomed. You may find a few comrades who are ready to shift along with you, but, if you take a look at history, changes always involve challenges.

It isn't always best to try to convince those who make the laws that your way is better. It's better to work with the people who desire the same changes as you do, because then that energy spreads. Any attempt to change the outer without changing the inner will always be subject to distortion on either side of the equation or situation.

The same thing is true with those who are changing while their families aren't. It's not always the goal to convince the people around you who don't agree with you that you're right. It's more important to find like-minded people to be with rather than trying to force change on those people who aren't really ready. Give your wisdom where it is welcome.

Q. YOU HEAR A LOT ABOUT "JOY" THESE DAYS. DOES JOY HAVE A CONNECTION TO ABUNDANCE OR PROSPERITY?

A. Joy is the state of natural abundance, of right action, and flow. It encompasses the heart, mind, and body being in full accordance with one another. Joy is active engagement, fully uncensored, watchful, observing, participating, absorbing, and releasing. It is more of a *function* than a state of mind—and it encompasses wonder, the delight of information, of intimacy, uncensored.

You could say that joy is a purpose, expectancy... a decision. You could also say that joy is a reminder of what is true. It is more than a feeling, but it encompasses feeling. It is more than an attitude—but it encompasses attitude. It is an *engagement with life.*

It is a decision because it is always present. It stands proud to fear, dissolves disillusion in the moment; it is a pride of God Source. It is intimately one with creation, therefore it is creative—it expects—it knows.

Joy is naturally discriminatory because it knows only the truth—the facts of creation. It is in the delight, the magnificence, the knowing—it is *All There Is*. Standing in joy is an active way to live, a conscious choice of alignment with truth, a daily activity, a presence in the moment, a deliberate focus, and a remembrance of God Source.

When all else seems to suggest the contrary, the nagging thoughts, the fearful futures, the panic of loving, joy comes and reminds, reassures, relaxes, re-empowers, laughs at ego and illusions and stands in the face of difficulties. Joy stands as it has always stood, and will always stand, ever present, ever true, ever God. It is "to open the wide wooden door, look out and see that the horizon is nothing but clear, blue skies." Above every cloud, are always blue skies! That is the constant.

As an adjunct to the topic of "Prosperity," I am including an article that I wrote some years ago after the conclusion in this book. (See "Symbolism in Your Everyday Life" on page 167.) Its focus is on developing the conscious awareness of connecting the outer events in your life to your inner belief systems, which often relate to our view of prosperity.

In this practice, you see that your outer world is a dreamscape of your thoughts and beliefs. Everything is "associative" in the sense that your beliefs and thoughts are what they are because of associations you have made in your mind with the experiences of your life. "Associative" means that your outer world is a symbolic representation of your inner world. Once you can "read" this symbolism, you can make choices that will truly change your experiences. In other words, you will become a "conscious chooser" as opposed to a "sleeping follower."

Messages from Mother Mary

Chapter 16

Messages from Mother Mary

In two group sessions in April 2012, Mother Mary came through the Records and spoke to us at length about the Divine Masculine and Feminine principles as they pertain to our world in this present time of change.

Standing behind her was a group of women whom Mary called "the Holy Women" of times past. Mary herself appeared as a woman-child of about 14 years of age. Her hair was medium brown and long, and her eyes were brown, soft and loving. She wore a dark blue jacket that radiated power, love and truth. She was short in height, yet "tall" in her presence.

Although appearing at this young age, her maturity and motherly love were evident. Perhaps the young age was to impart her "innocence" which was also obvious. Although innocent, she was not naïve, as her knowledge of God Source and the universe was very much apparent. I could feel the balance within her—her loving heart mixed with high intelligence, her gentleness mixed with clear and direct information, her humor mixed with seriousness. She asked me to impart her messages in this book.

Mother Mary:

It is important to realize that the "Holy Women" were and are a big part of the plan for Earth. Their presence has upheld the feminine principle throughout time. Without it, there would be no Earth, no life, no co-creation or indeed, no pro-creation. Many Holy Women sat back in silence while they nurtured, cared for, counseled and encouraged. They prepared food, washed clothes, bathed children and men, smiled graciously, read and told stories, tended the sick, mended the wounded, prayed and loved ceaselessly.

They were master healers, knowing the science of herbs and plants. They performed rituals under the Sun and Moon, donating their energy to the continuation of life and the living. They danced and sang in celebration, praising the living universe and the Source of all creation. Without them there would be no harvest, no fruition of seeds, no joy of birth, no comfort at death. Without them, there would be no life. They deserve their recognition and honor, and this must carry forward into this present and future time.

The imbalance between the masculine and feminine principles has been in place for too many centuries. I am saddened by the degree of fragmentation of these principles in your world. When these principles are out of balance, deprivation and poverty ensue. Pole shifts result due to the extreme polarization of these principles. Before the split into polar opposites, the male and female were one *tonal* harmonic. Pole shifts were not necessary. It is worthy to note, however, that at this present time, the polarization has not caused the "scales to tip" into a pole shift.

We were all originally androgynous in our nature, carrying the balance of the Divine Masculine and Divine Feminine within us. This was when we were living in Paradise because *we* were each, a living Paradise. We were in harmony within and so also with our environment. Co-creation with our Creator was natural and obvious.

You can consider that the Divine Masculine and Divine Feminine are the out-breath and in-breath of Creation as well as the clockwise and counterclockwise motion of the cosmos. When there is distortion in these flows, upheaval and suffering are the result.

Each of us is a divine parent to ourselves, the Earth, and to one another. We have been "out of phase" with our androgyny for many eons. It is why history keeps repeating itself, why you do not see lasting change when attempts to return to our Paradise state are in motion. It is why the momentum never reaches the balance necessary to shift humanity into harmony and cooperation. When men can once again be divine mothers and women can once again be divine fathers, then we will have a chance.

It is the Divine Masculine and Divine Feminine *within each individual* that must be recognized, forgiven and united.

Soul-mate and twin-flame relationships are attempts to heal the division between male and female energies. That many twin flames are reuniting now is part of the plan to bring forth this inner reunion and communion. They carry the *memory* of these principles in perfect balance and also carry the original tonal coding to reactivate this reunion.

This is not a time to be complacent. More than ever do you have to come to inner balance to hold the increasing frequency of Light that is being made available amidst the chaos. None can afford to sit back and ignore the constant attacks on your personal freedom and right to choose. The shift must come from within you first to see the change in outer events. *At this time, questions to Mother Mary were introduced.*

Q. HOW DO WE ATTAIN MALE/FEMALE BALANCE ON EARTH?

A. You can have group meditations where each individual meditates on the Sun and Moon within themselves or explore breath—its inward and outward flow in silence, in listening, in rhythm. You can study the movements of clockwise and counterclockwise spirals.

Clockwise spirals bring *down* electrical properties from the Sun and put this *into* the Earth or a life form. Counterclockwise spirals bring magnetic properties *up* from the Earth into the surface of the Earth or into a life form. The male/female balance must be achieved on a personal level first, and is affected by how a person is using their Sun and Moon energies.

All suggestions above can be done individually and privately and should be. You can also meditate on *me* and on the Star of Bethlehem. This will awaken the memory of the Divine Masculine and Feminine within your heart. The Star of Bethlehem is one of the original Paradise planets.

It is less about what we can do to shift an outward event on Earth and more about getting people to meditate on these principles within themselves. The Sun represents the masculine principle of action, dynamism, extroversion, vitality, the conscious mind, electricity and regeneration, while the Moon represents the feminine principle of introversion, nurturing, subconscious activity, self-reflection, calmness, gestation, magnetism, emotion and depth. Each must take a look at how well these forces are utilized and balanced within.

It is obvious on Earth that the masculine principle has become extreme. Because of this, it has taken on a negative distortion with war, aggression, tyranny, slavery, domination over others and the misuse of power and control. The widespread misuse of authority and suppression of the freedom that our Creator gave each of us is an abomination of great magnitude.

The suppression and invalidation of the feminine principle has run rampant for millennia. You will see no change in the world if these principles are not brought into harmony, correction, and balance.

If a group of people meditate for a better world but within themselves there is still a deep polarity or imbalance between *inner* male and female, there will be no permanent change in the outer world. What we see in the world is always a mirror of ourselves.

Men need to know about their hearts. They have been deprived of their wholeness by the distortions in the patriarchal system they have been reared into. Women have been suppressed and deprived of their wholeness as well. Heart energy is whole, not singular or strictly individual.

Q. COULD YOU TELL US ABOUT A PARTICULAR HOLY WOMAN?

A. No, I cannot choose one over the other at this time. Honor all women, not just Mary the Mother of Jesus.

Q. WOULD YOU MOTHER MARY, LIKE TO HEAR A STORY THAT RELATES TO YOUR ANSWER?

A. Yes!

Participant: An anthropologist proposed a game to children in an African tribe. He put a basket full of fruit near a tree and told the children that whoever got to the tree first would win the fruits. When he told them to run, they all took each other's hands and ran together, then sat together enjoying the fruits.

When the anthropologist asked them why they had run as one, since one child could have been the winner and had all the fruit for himself, they said: "Ubuntu! How can one of us be happy if the rest of us are sad?" ("Ubuntu" in Xhosa culture means: "I am because we are.")

Q. JESUS MUST HAVE REQUIRED A PURE VEHICLE TO BE BORN
THROUGH TO COMPLETE HIS MISSION. CAN YOU TELL US ABOUT
YOUR "ANCESTRY" OR "LINEAGE"?

A. I have an ancient lineage in that I come from the Spheres of Golden
Light close to the Throne of Source. When in the form of a golden sphere,
the form one takes on or *is*, is more of a "Sound tone" form. As a "being,"
you would carry a certain tonal frequency as your "identity." This is where I
and others of my ancient galactic family have our origin—in the Golden
Sound Tone Spheres close to Source.

We are not native to Earth. We come into particular planetary systems
to bring ascension codes to the gene pool there. Some of those codes could
be Christ codes, Light and Sound codes, or particular God codes.

These codes could also be called, "pure tonal frequencies." The purpose
is always to "resurrect" a system to a higher God awareness by putting
these codes into the gene pool so they become available to the *entire* race of
beings on any given planet. You could call it a "savior mission," and there
have been many of them throughout history, not limited strictly to the Earth.
Some have called us "Star beings," and this would be true also.

Many would also like to call me a "Melchizedek," but I am more distin-
guished by the carrying of the golden tonal rings and as one of the original
Golden Spheres of Light off Source.

When we come into a planetary system and take on the life form of that
system, we bring with us certain tonal frequencies that will uplift that system, and we make them available physically. Three quarters of all humans
are missing tones, similar to missing keys on a piano. It is difficult to be
harmonious with missing tones!

Reincarnation allows a slow process of rebuilding missing tones, but it
is a very slow process of "ascending back up the ladder" if you will.
Depending on what a soul does and chooses in each lifetime, it will either
build up tonal frequencies or fragment itself further.

Many of the "new" children that are coming to Earth are coming from
realms that have more tones available. They are able to carry these tones
with them through the combined *biologies* of their parents. Thus more pure
tones are put into the gene pool where they can uplift the ancestry of both

parents backwards and forwards. They do this by activating tonal codes and keys at the soul level of both parents.

Twin-flame relationships coming together now are also helping to bring tonal frequencies together to create the harmonic resonance of wholeness.

There is no "magic pill" that will reinstate the missing tones, no fast track biologically or on the soul level, but there are more and more Light codes coming in from Source Creator at this time to help accelerate the process. Some have called this "the Quickening."

Source sends Light codes throughout the universe to allow all life forms to activate and actualize greater potential and repair missing tonal frequencies. This usually occurs in cycles only because certain cosmic doorways need to be opened for these codes to be able to come in.

Q. WHAT IS A GALACTIC SOUL FAMILY?

A. A Galactic Soul Family is a group of beings from the same original collective that travel together for specific purposes, usually originating from other universes or systems.

Q. DID YOU HAVE OTHER LIVES ON EARTH?

A. I was an Atlantean, an Egyptian and a Native American. As an Atlantean, I was not native to many Earth lives at that time. It was a time of high spiritual and technological advancement. Jesus shared that lifetime also. In Egypt, I was a "normal" young girl playing in the streets. In my teenage years, I became an adept and learned much about the male and female principles. As a Native American, I became known as White Buffalo Calf Woman.

These lives helped me build soul strength. All powerful people build up their soul's strength through multiple life experiences.

Q. DID YOU REALLY APPEAR TO BERNADETTE AT LOURDES?

A. Yes, I appeared as a young girl to Bernadette at Lourdes so as to not scare her, much the same as I am showing myself to you. The land area that is Lourdes is a sacred area that we passed through when we traveled through France after the crucifixion. The Earth grids cross there, and an intersection of realities occurs. So miracles can happen there, which is why I chose to appear there. It was a desire of mine to bring many people there so they could find comfort, peace and healing. There are several other powerful areas in that region, but most are in the mountains and inaccessible to large groups of people. This is not the Catholic story, but it is the true one.

I chose Bernadette because her heart was pure and she was stubborn enough to stand up to the attention that would follow. She always told the truth about what she saw at the apparitions. I also chose her because she, too, is from the Golden Spheres of Light, so she is my galactic "sister."

Bernadette also had lifetimes in Atlantis and Egypt, as well as numerous Native American lives, and she was also a Basque. I bestowed much grace on Bernadette and allowed her to remember her visions of Paradise. I would have given her miracles if she had asked, but it was not her way. She prayed to suffer like Jesus, but God does not ask for suffering. God's desire is only love.

Q. YOU MENTIONED THAT THE HOLY WOMEN OF THE PAST WERE MASTERS IN THE USE OF HERBS. WHAT CAN YOU TELL US ABOUT THE IMPORTANCE OF HERBS?

A. Herbs carry the feminine principle throughout nature. They are like mother's milk for the Earth and her people. Their use is widespread and provides nourishment, balance, healing and inspiration. I would include the use of flower essences in the same category.

The imbalanced masculine energy throughout the history of Earth has killed women for the use of herbs for healing, thus suppressing the feminine principle in Nature. The banning of herbs in this time period is another attempt to continue this suppression of the feminine. If it succeeds, your people and planet will fall into another dark period in history. You must not accept this. If your perception were whole, you would see and hear the kingdom of nature as the tonal harmonic that it is.

Each chakra in the human anatomy is also a tone of creation. Your ears are external chakras that create a triangulation with the pineal gland in the brain. You could call this triangulation the "capstone" to your bodily ascension vehicle.

I will reveal more to you at a future time on this subject.

Our Future Selves

Chapter 17

Our Future Selves

Our inquiry is to learn about our "Future Selves"—*Who* are they? *Where* are they? And *what* are they doing?

As I was saying the prayer, the room became crowded with beings. I didn't know who they were, but they all looked the same—all white light beings filling up the room. Were they our Future Selves? Let's find out...

Q. ARE WE LOOKING 10, 50, 100 YEARS OR EVEN 1,000 INCARNATIONS DOWN THE ROAD? ARE WE LOOKING AT OUR ASCENDED SELVES?

A. Let's look at the beings that came in first to see who they are. Yes, they are our Future Selves, but also some of our galactic soul family. They are Home in Source but are also here at the same time.

When you ask which selves we're looking at, the beings in this room want us to ask some general questions first. They're here to give us information. They're coming in as a collective and are more than the number of us in this room. They are all very tall and spirit in form—very light, bright beings. What they're saying to me is: "If you knew they were *you*, what would you really want to know?"

Q. DO THEY COME FROM PARALLEL REALITIES?

A. The image they're giving me is like a star burst. Imagine the center point in a star burst and everything expanding from that and going in multi-dimensional directions. So instead of parallel, think multi-*dimensional*.

Q. ARE THEY EMBODIED OR JUST ENERGY?

A. They can take on any type of "body" they desire. They are not limited. When they "travel," they just "pop in." I don't feel any kind of a distance. I do not see them limited by space and time or dimensions as we perceive them. Because we are having this topic tonight, they just "popped in."

Q. HAVE WE EXPERIENCED THEM ALREADY BEFORE?

A. You have memory of them, and when you're sleeping you make visits to your Future Selves all the time.

Q. DOES THAT MEAN OUR FUTURE SELVES HAVE LIVED BEFORE? OR IS IT A COMPLETELY NEW EXPERIENCE?

A. They are not new, that's for sure; they feel *always*, like they have never *not* been. I can't see a time when they weren't there. It feels that it's the *us* that never left Creator or "Home." They are a part that is very close to Source and has never left that Light. Having said that, they can travel anywhere they want, pop in and pop out. A *thought* makes them appear and disappear.

Q. DO YOU EXPERIENCE YOUR FUTURE SELF IN DYING?

A. Not necessarily, in terms of that aspect of you. It isn't necessarily a given that when you die you would merge with that aspect of you.

Q. IT SOUNDS TO ME THAT OUR FUTURE SELVES ARE VERY MUCH "ETHERIC" OR "LIGHT BEINGS" AS OPPOSED TO HOW WE PERCEIVE OURSELVES NOW IN 3-D. I WONDER WHAT MY NEXT FUTURE SELF, OR INCARNATION IS GOING TO LOOK LIKE? WILL OUR FUTURE SELVES BE TANGIBLE OR INTANGIBLE?

A. The aspect of us that has shown up here is very intangible. The truth is that we have many other selves existing right now in many other dimensions and "parallel" dimensions. We have multiple selves that are living active lives, as you would consider yourself doing here. Yet they all feel as if they are right here, right now, at the same time.

Our Future Selves have shown up tonight because we asked about them. They are very "etheric" or "light," not solid, as we perceive ourselves in 3-D and would not be having "incarnations."

Q. CAN WE UNDERSTAND MORE OF OUR NEXT INCARNATION?

A. They're not showing Future Selves to me in that type of vertical picture, like rungs on a ladder. They're saying we have *multidimensional selves.* Think "spherical" in terms of yourselves, not linear.

Some are at certain levels of densification, and some are lighter. Our "collective selves" are all here right now. They all exist *now.* What they're showing me is that you can't focus on one self because they are *all* part of your collective whole, and they all contribute to your particular essence. You aren't an individual really, in this sense. Your own self—your *real* self—has many beings that go with it. You can ask questions about them.

What I'm finding interesting here is that the light beings who are here tonight are calling themselves our *Future Selves*. Let me ask why, because I feel like they have always been here.

They're saying that's where we are going back to. Even though they were there at the beginning, it seems our perceptions have left and gone off on this journey, and now when we go back, we go back to being that self.

That's why they're calling themselves *Future Selves*, even though we *technically* never left them, but we have left them in a sense. They are the part of us that pulls us Home. That's your *real* Future Self—it's the self that's already Home, pulling us back.

They call themselves "the future" because they see your entire journey from a vantage point where they are watching all your multi-dimensional selves all at once. They are aware of it all; they're aware of the journey, and the choices, and they're just waiting, but not with any sense of urgency. From their perspective, time really doesn't make a difference. I feel very clearly that they are the whole of you—you feel it as the part that pulls you back Home.

Q. IF TIME DOESN'T MAKE ANY DIFFERENCE TO THEM, WHAT'S THE BIG HULLABALOO ABOUT 2012 ENERGIES AND TIME CYCLES?

A. They are saying that in the big picture, it doesn't matter. In terms of the journey back, parts of us perceive ourselves in time. When we get into time, suddenly there are cycles and perception of space and distance. But outside of time, where they exist, it doesn't matter. That "us," or our Future Selves, is not affected by time at all, but because we're "down here" in a *perception* of time; this is how we relate, how we define things.

Q. SO IF WE WERE IN TUNE WITH OUR FUTURE SELVES, WOULD THERE STILL BE A NEED TO ENGAGE IN ALL THIS?

A. There is a way to connect directly Home.

Q. SO OUR CONCERN ABOUT THE NEXT LIFETIME AND THE NEXT RUNG ON THE LADDER SHOULD BE NO CONCERN TO US AT ALL?

A. When we really want to go Home we will, and that's the answer. The truth is we actually use time as a way to *not* have to go back Home right away, even though we say we want to go back. The truth is that if you really wanted to go back, you'd be back.

Q. SO HOW DO YOU ACHIEVE A DEEPER CONNECTION?

A. The question they're putting back to us is do you want to go Home? The straight line that I'm seeing and the fast track Home only happens when you actually say "I'm ready to go Home." That statement begins to bypass all your other lives and makes them unnecessary. This is because it "forgives" or "releases" the past and brings everything to completion in an instant.

The issue is that most of us don't really want to go Home. Most of us, as much as we complain about our lives, are attached to them. Playing with form and dimension, having experiences with places we all invented is fun for most of us. All these places, all these dimensions, even the planes of existence after death, are actually all invented by us.

The place where Source *is* doesn't concern itself with any of that. Your Future Self will interact in your life as you need it to, but their main purpose is not as a guide, but to collapse the perception of time and space in your consciousness.

Even though I perceive our Future Selves "in a place," they're really everywhere, similar to how God Source is everywhere. To connect with them means you need to be willing to have time collapse in your perception of yourself and the many other "lives" you live and have lived. This implies giving up ego identifications or the perception of yourself as a *person,* rather than the eternal Spirit from Source that you are.

In Truth, the idea that we are on a *journey* Home is an illusion. There is no journey really—only the decision on when you want to go Home.

Our collective perception has invented time and space as well as the idea that we have different selves. The whole multidimensional aspect of it all is a product of our own making. There's no judgment about it. Your Future Self is untouchable, unaffected by what we have made up with our minds. It cannot be destroyed, always was, always will be, just like Source.

Q. IS THERE A WINDOW OF TIME OR PORTAL THAT IS COLLAPSING?

A. There is no portal "out there" —it is all *in* your consciousness already. When you are really ready, you will experience time collapsing in your consciousness. Portals, in the external sense, are still part of the illusion we have all invented.

Now think about all your experiences of being other people in other lives, of being who you perceive yourself to be in *this* life, of being one or more of your multidimensional selves now, of wondering what they might be doing in the next 20 years, of being on your own path in this present time, of wanting to keep experiencing 2012 and beyond, of enjoying your grandchildren and your relationships. When I put it to you that way, do you really want all of that collapsed? Most people don't.

(See also "Q. What does 2012 have to do with it all?" on page 83.)

Q. IS A PERSON WHO IS CONSIDERING SUICIDE READY TO RELINQUISH ALL EXPERIENCES?

A. The consciousness that commits suicide is still entrapped in perception of their reality. If they weren't entrapped in perception, they wouldn't want to commit suicide. The fact that they are perceiving their reality a certain way, and think that if they commit suicide they'll be in a different place, have a different mind, *etc.*, shows you they are still in the realm of identifying themselves as a personality.

(See "Q. Could you explain more about how we are pulling in negative interference as a part of us?" on page 47.)

Participant: I can see the difficulty that I certainly have, and perhaps I speak for other people in terms of being caught in 3-D—it seems impossible to understand something that's in another dimension, because we need to be in it in order to experience it. So for me to understand the concept of being a Light Being as my Future Self, I'm finding that very difficult. It raises a question for me in terms of your saying we created this reality, and I can believe and understand that, but then a question that's puzzled me for a long time is...

Q. DID EXTRATERRESTRIALS CREATE US IN THEIR PERCEPTION, OR ARE WE CREATING THEM IN OUR PERCEPTION?

A. It's all part of the same illusion. ETs are not outside of the illusion, so the answer is: "yes" and "yes"—we create them and they create us—it's all part of the illusion. That you are a "separate self" is what the real illusion is.

However, if you were suddenly to decide to go Home, don't make the mistake of thinking that *you* would be no more. Going Home is not about annihilation—it is about *expansion*, about being *All That Is*. In the big picture, we look like little puppets that are doing our little dance and doing our little dramas. There's no judgment around it—we can play this as long as we want to play this—as long as we desire to have a separate experience.

There will come a time when you will be ready to go Home, and when you are ready, you'll go Home. There are no rules in the sense that you have to endure all these experiences in order to *get* Home. From Source's point of view there are no lessons to learn, no enlightenment to practice for X amount of life times, *etc.* It's like Dorothy in the Wizard of Oz realizing she had always been able to go Home whenever she wanted to—she just didn't know it. She always had her ruby slippers on!

Play as long as you want in the playing field. The only limiting thing I see is perception. In other words, perception is the thing that makes you feel like you're in hell or heaven, or a little of both. When people get "trapped" in places, they're trapped because of their perception.

For example, let's say you die and find yourself in an undesirable plane of existence and you don't see any way out. Your perception created that field of existence in the first place, so there's *always* a way out, but if you don't *know* there is, you'll stay in that plane indefinitely.

It's all perception, and seeing it from this vantage point, we're just children in a dream playing around. All the things we worry about and take seriously, and even all the experiences of birth and death that we have, none of them *have* to happen. This is why you're really in a field of unlimited possibilities in terms of what you decide to perceive.

I still have to say, that as much as we think we are in all these different planes of existence, the truth is that none of them are Home. They're still the dream fields, the playing fields.

(See also "Q. Will we be seeing more ETs? Will there be full disclosure?" on page 105.)

Q. IS THERE ACTUALLY ANY POINT THEN IN OUR ASKING ANY MORE QUESTIONS? (LAUGHTER)

A. It can be fun to know what other aspects of "you" are doing, which helps you know what you've been creating. The real value in it is from the point of perception of where you're at, because no one in this room is ready to go Home. We're all having too much fun, and even in your worst nightmare you're still having fun.

Q. WHY SEPARATE FROM SOURCE AND THE UNIFIED SELF IN THE FIRST PLACE?

A. Well first of all, you didn't actually separate from anything. The perception that you did is an illusion as well. It was only a thought, but a thought similar to wanting to know the "all" of us. It's a very difficult thing to say, but it was just an instant thought that produced this phenomenon. I don't see it as any sort of a rebellion or of wanting to turn away from Source. It could have been as simple as a thought of "what else is there?" where suddenly this field of all possibilities is created.

Thought itself starts creating things, like a snowball effect. Suddenly there are more thoughts and other thoughts, and before you know it, there's unlimited thought and potential.

Those unlimited thoughts keep multiplying off themselves to a point where we forgot we were thinking. We forgot the original thought, and now we believe that all these *effects* from our thoughts are the reality.

We forgot that we're the *thinker*, that we're the being that's thinking. Now we're caught up in the effect! We think the *effect* is us, even though it's *all* us. We are thinking that the small self—the effect of thought—Is us. We have forgotten the Future Self or everything self that started thinking in the first place. None of us has really left Home. Each of us is still our original self.

Q. CAN YOU GET IN A POSITION WHERE YOU'RE MAKING A CHOICE TO GO OR NOT GO HOME?

A. You're always in a choice whether to go or not go. However, no one is ever completely choosing to go, because if you were, you'd be there.

Now if you think about it for a moment, everyone's hung up in having experiences. Even sitting here in your body and saying you want to have an experience of Home, you want to feel connected to Home—you could have a feeling or a sense of it.

But it's always going to be temporary as long as you want to still experience bodies and forms and dimensions. That's why it's temporary, that's why you never really *maintain* or *sustain* an experience of any kind really, positive or negative. The truth is that none of that will ever last; it will only last as long as your perception wants to perceive it.

Participant: You once said you had an out-of-body experience, and what brought you back was the thought, "Oh I'm not going to be able to get back to my children," and suddenly you were back in your body.

Yes, I actually *dematerialized*, I wasn't out of my body. I dematerialized and saw my body turn into molecules of Light. The concern for my children instantly put me back into my body.

Q. IF WE MAKE THE CHOICE NOW TO GO HOME, COULD WE STILL COME BACK TO OUR CHILDREN, OR WOULD WE LOSE OUR CONNECTION TO THEM?

A. You don't ever lose the connection to anyone or anything. If you decide to go Home, you are saying you are finished with the playing field of separation, with the *idea* of it and the *belief* in it. A shift would most likely occur in your mind and perception first. At the point where you return to Spirit, you would be Spirit. Could you ever materialize again to your children? Yes, but you may not have the same form.

Q. SO I DECIDE TO GO HOME, WHICH IS BACK AT THE "SHORE," FOR EXAMPLE. MY KIDS ARE STILL WAY OUT THERE IN THE MIDDLE OF THE OCEAN WITH A LIFE BUOY. WHEN I'M HOME, DO I WANT TO STAY HOME? OR DO I SAY, "HEY I'VE GOT TO SWIM BACK OUT THERE, BECAUSE MY KIDS ARE OUT THERE.

A. You can do whatever you want. If you want to come back into time, you can project yourself back into time. The problem is when people project themselves back into time; they are now in a field of memory. So what you might want to say is time is memory, time is the collection of memory.

Once you project yourself back into the field of time, chances are you won't remember Home. That's what happens. You're in the field of time, which is the field of memories, and that's a field of perception. Once you're immersed in this field, and you step back into time and into perception, you can see how easy it would be to just get lost in it and to perceive yourself as the "small self" once again. Once you're involved in it, it is difficult to remember your Future Self.

Q. SO IF I DID GO HOME, I WOULDN'T WANT TO COME BACK?

A. That's true, but it's so hard to explain. A thought will create a perception, and a perception will create an experience and a reality. If you ever *really* wanted to go Home and wanted to be done playing the game entirely, you would most likely not want any more lifetimes in dimensionality.

Now think about it, a lot of us are hung up in "What planet did I come from? What star system? What lifetimes have I yet to live? I hope I never come back to Earth, or maybe I'll go to Venus next time." With all the desires we're having, the dramas we're playing in, and the experiences we get to have, there really aren't many of us who ever really say, "I'm ready to go Home," certainly not in the "Home" sense we're talking about here.

Q. IF TIME COLLAPSED, WOULD YOUR PAST BE GONE?

A. No. If you went Home you would know everything all at once. You don't lose anything—you expand *into and become* everything. You become more aware, not less aware. You'd see it all—your children, the dramas, the multi-dimensional selves. The difference is that you would see it all as a playing field on which you are no longer interested in playing.

The difference is your awareness that the others are all out there still playing in the illusion. Until they are ready to stop playing in the illusion and go Home, they won't be aware of you watching them play. At any point you could project yourself back into the field of time, back into any kind of time reality or any type of dimension, if you so chose. You could just materialize at will or decide to come in as a baby to a different family, depending on your purpose for coming back into this dimension.

Our Future Selves are here with us now because we asked the question, "Who are our Future Selves?" They have "popped in" to our dimensional space to answer our question. That thought, that inquiry, brought them here.

Where the error has happened, if I can call it an error, is that once you're projected into a dimension, that dimension suddenly becomes reality to you, and then you perceive yourself differently. You perceive "Now I'm in 'x' dimension; these are the rules, the laws of this dimension." You're so immersed in it that you perceive it as real and fixed and therefore limited with certain boundaries.

This is the difficulty—we're all trying to get out of our belief in limitations. The truth is any type of experience is just a thought. But once you're immersed in it all and you have and *feel* an experience, that experience is now *real* to you. Experience now becomes your perception of your identity, and you have now forgotten who you are in truth. Still, your *real* self is still Home, looking at it all and knowing this aspect of you is out there on this playing field.

Q. YOU HAVE SAID THAT OUR FUTURE SELVES CAME INTO THE ROOM. HOW CAN WE MAKE A CONNECTION WITH THEM? CAN WE ASK OUR FUTURE SELVES TO HELP US GET OUT OF THE ILLUSION OF TIME?

A. Yes, that's exactly what our Future Selves are saying: "What do you want to ask of us? Whatever you say you want of us, we will give you that experience."

Q. WE'RE TAUGHT THAT WE CAN ASK FOR HELP, BUT IT'S ALWAYS OUTSIDE OF OURSELVES FROM SEPARATE BEINGS, SUCH AS THIS ARCHANGEL OR THAT SAINT. ARE THESE BEINGS ALSO WHERE OUR FUTURE SELVES ARE, OR IS THAT A WHOLE SEPARATE BELIEF SYSTEM?

A. They would also be part of the illusory perception of identity.

Q. SO THEREFORE ANYTHING WITH A SAINT NAME ON IT OR ANYTHING WITH AN ARCHANGEL IS ALSO ALL PERCEPTION?

A. I have to be clear here. At the level of the Future Self that is Home—it is making no judgment. If you want to believe in an angel or a being that is going to do something for you, you can. There's nothing wrong with it, but realize how powerful your mind is. If you can call on a being whom you perceive to be more powerful than you, and you believe that it will provide assistance for you, then it will. But is it really an outside being that is pro-viding the assistance, or the belief of your powerful mind that's doing it? Or are you tuning into another aspect of *yourself* who is your own angelic self?

We all make the mistake of thinking it's a long way Home. We think that this journey is about *time*, its lessons and the accumulation of wisdom. In Truth, you don't have to do anything to get Home except know that you're still there, as your Future Self. Like Dorothy with her ruby slip-pers—she was in Oz having all these experiences; she's with the wizard; she's in the Emerald City, and she's being poisoned by poppies, the witch is after her, *etc.* She's on this journey having this experience, and then there's a point where she says, "I just want to go Home." Glinda comes and tells her she always had the ability to go Home. All she needed was the desire.

"There's no place like Home."

Play as long as you want, but you could do it a lot more joyfully if you wouldn't take it all so seriously.

Q. SO YOU DON'T HAVE TO DO ANYTHING—YOU JUST BECOME YOUR FUTURE SELF, AND DROP ALL THOUGHTS OF EVERYTHING ELSE?

A. Yes, that's it.

Q. IF SOMEONE TAKES A MIND-ALTERING SUBSTANCE TO TRY TO GET INTO THAT PLACE THAT FEELS LIKE HOME, THEY FEEL THAT THEY ARE SERIOUSLY HOME. WHY AREN'T THEY HOME?

A. Because a *vision* of Home is not the same as *being* Home. They are not really Home. The truth is the chemical, at its best, can only create a mirror *reflection* of Home. It isn't the *thing*, the state of actually *being* your Future Self. The chemical is not the thing, it's a reflection.

You can take a drug that might open a part of your brain and produce certain chemicals, and those chemicals would give you a vision. It could be any kind of vision really, but that vision at its best is still only a reflection of something that is somewhere else. It isn't the same as being there or being "It."

People who take drugs to produce an altered state are still invested in their physical identities. They wouldn't be taking the drugs if they didn't already perceive themselves as a person in a body who needs to take a drug to have an expanded vision.

Q. SO THEY'RE NOT HAVING A REAL EXPERIENCE AT ALL?

A. No, they're not having a real experience of Home. They're having a mirrored reflection or temporary experience of an alternate reality. The fact that the experience is temporary proves it is just a perception.

Q. AREN'T THEY CHOOSING TO BE HOME WHILE IN THAT SPACE?

A. No, they are still in perception because when you truly want to be Home, it is an actual happening—not a disguised experience of it.

Q. I HAD A MEMORY OF DYING IN A PAST LIFE. DID I DIE?

A. So you were remembering a past life—in essence reliving a memory.

Q. WHAT WOULD A FUTURE LIFE BE LIKE IF WE WERE TO STAY IN THE GAME?

A. If you decide to stay in the game, your future lives (your next incarnation) will be as you make them. You are already living all your lives right now. Think about the idea that there is no "next incarnation," but only the choice to *focus your awareness* in a life that is already going on right now. We just keep recycling our awareness into various lives we are already living and calling that "a new life."

Q. CAN SOMEBODY ELSE PREVENT YOU FROM GOING HOME BY WANTING TO KEEP YOU HERE?

A. If you were really deciding to go Home nobody could stop you. It is true that we're all in this collective illusion and we're all agreeing to it on this level, but when you are really finished with the illusion, you will be.

Q. CAN PSYCHIC CORDS OR OTHER BEINGS OR PERSONS PREVENT OUR GOING HOME?

A. Nobody can stop you if you really want to go Home. It's *your* decision. Psychic cords exist between people, but there is usually some unconscious agreement between both or all parties concerned for them to be in place.

Participant: It begs the next question, though, about enlightened beings that are on the planet at this point in this illusion. We regard them as enlightened simply because they're pulling great wisdom out of the ethers and giving us a similar type of concept of God and how to go Home. A lot of them are saying we now have the opportunity to create Heaven on Earth or that we now have the opportunity to have our thoughts manifest whatever we like and to stay focused on the positive.

Q. IF ENLIGHTENED BEINGS ARE REALLY ENLIGHTENED, WHY AREN'T THEY FOCUSING ON MAKING US CHOOSE TO GO HOME?

A. Because there isn't any right or wrong, and they do understand perception. What they're doing is trying to free up your perceptions—possibly to move you into a "happy perception" to show you that you have personal power. The choice to go Home only comes after you're really tired of the game and all its experiences. It is also a realization that only real joy is union with God or your real self.

Until then, we will try all kinds of other things to achieve what can only be achieved within. There are teachings that basically say you can go Home at any time. Just decide to say yes, ask and you shall receive. Those teachings have been around for a long time, but the point is we're really not ready to give up the dream game of experiences.

A being who is truly enlightened knows about Home. There can be beings or teachers who have gained greater experiences or awarenesses than us, but it doesn't mean they are enlightened. They can stimulate us to move beyond our limited perceptions and prove to us that we are not limited or finite, but ultimately it is you who must make your own decisions.

Q. I ALWAYS BELIEVED THAT ALL ROADS LEAD HOME ULTIMATELY, NO MATTER WHAT YOU BELIEVE IN. ARE YOU SAYING THEN, THAT A LOT OF THEM MIGHT JUST KEEP YOU IN THE PERCEPTION GAME EVEN LONGER?

A. Whether you think you're in Heaven or Hell, it is still in perception. As long as you perceive your body as your self, you're in perception. You know if somebody got into Satanism, for example, and they spent 80 years of their life in there, no matter what it is, it's still perception.

Q. WHEN YOU'RE IN THE GAME, ARE YOU IN CAUSE AND EFFECT?

A. Yes, cause and effect came into being once the belief in separation occurred.

Q. SO WITH ALL THESE OTHER LIVES THAT WE'RE LIVING AT THE SAME TIME, HOW CAN OUR FUTURE SELF REALLY HELP US WHEN WE'RE ONLY ONE ASPECT?

A. Good question! Everything about you, everything you've experienced, the perceptions and even the memory of Home is here within you, within all aspects of you. The thing about all the other selves is that every one of them at some point is going to choose to go Home.

Now you are becoming aware of your Future Self who *is* Home and has always been Home. With this awareness, you can now choose to go Home to your Future Self, or you can choose to stay in the game longer. Your Future Self is here to help you should you decide you are done with the game.

If you didn't become aware of your Future Self today, you'd never know there was a *choice* that could be made to opt out of the illusory playing field.

Q. SO, IT'S UP TO ME AT THE END OF THE DAY?

A. It's up to you at the end of the day to decide for the aspect of yourself you are in right now.

Q. BUT IF WE DECIDE AS ONE OF THE ASPECTS THAT WE WANT TO GO HOME, ARE THOSE OTHER SELVES AUTOMATICALLY ALL INCLUDED?

A. No.

Q. SO WHAT HAPPENS THEN? DOES ONLY THIS ASPECT DISAPPEAR FROM THE ILLUSION?

A. Yes, It's just going right Home.

Q. SO THE OTHERS ARE REALLY ON THEIR OWN?

A. They're in their own *perception* of being on their own. But remember, none of us have really left Home. We just *think* we have. When one aspect of you chooses to awaken from the dream, it will. The others will awaken as they are ready. Your choice to return Home will affect your other selves on some level. All are safe. You could have 10,000 other selves out there that are all in perception, and are all experiencing themselves. You may have some here, you may have some on Venus, you may have one on Saturn, and you may have 50 more on Earth.

Now they're all in their little collective illusion as long as they perceive themselves as separate persons or beings. But there will be a point where every one of those selves, of their own choice, will say, "I'm ready to go Home." They will one day realize who they are.

Think of your Future Self that is with you now as

a) The "you" that has never left Home and

b) The "yous" that have returned Home after playing in the illusion fields.

The selves of you that have individuated and who still want to play in illusion will one day decide to go Home. When each individuation returns, it becomes one with its Future Self. Think of it like a star going back to a star cluster. Suddenly you're not in the sky "alone" anymore because you've gone Home to the cluster, who are *all* you, as you were in the beginning.

Every action and choice that every self does influences all the others in some way. If you decide to go Home, it doesn't mean that all the others go Home at the same time. It means that because you've gone Home, it's now in their *memory*. It's in their microcosm that a piece of them went Home—so that memory is there now. That means there is a greater chance that they'll be aware of that, and they'll choose it when they're ready.

Q. BUT WHY WOULD THE "YOU" THAT MADE THE DECISION TO GO HOME CARE WHETHER THE OTHER "YOUS" HAVE DECIDED OR NOT, IF YOU'RE IN BLISS AT HOME?

A. You don't really care if they want to play in the illusion, but you're aware of it all. The only "tragedy" in this is that we get all caught up in believing that our perceptions and illusions are *real*. We go through all this pain and suffering, we cause ourselves and others pain and suffering—all due to our belief that we are a small self with no power.

Q. YOU SAID EARLIER THAT IT'S ALL THOUGHT AND WE ARE ORIGINAL THOUGHT. SO WHERE DO EMOTIONS COME FROM?

A. Emotions come from preconceived ideas and beliefs. All emotion comes from perception. However you connect or react has to do with your own perceptions and beliefs.

Q. WHEN ONE OF OUR ASPECTS GAINS AN UNDERSTANDING OR GIFT, WOULD OUR OTHER SELVES ALSO HAVE THOSE GIFTS, AND WOULD THEY BE USING THEM?

A. Yes, they could be.

Q. LET'S SAY I HAVE AN ASPIRATION TO BE A GREAT ARTIST, BUT I LACK THE ABILITY, OR I HAVE LOW SELF-ESTEEM, SO I'M NOT AN ARTIST IN THIS LIFETIME. IN MY NEXT LIFE, WOULD IT BE LIKELY THAT I COULD BE A GREAT ARTIST?

A. You can if you desire it, but your next life isn't in the future. It's already going on in some other dimensional space right now. Because of that you could choose to focus on it *now* and become a great artist in *this* particular awareness.

No matter what anyone says to you, it's still *you* that ultimately decides what's going to be your "future." "Future" only implies that which is not yet self-realized.

Q. IN THIS ILLUSORY REALITY, I DOUBT MYSELF A LOT. I'M WANDERING, AND I DON'T EXPECT TO GO BACK HOME. HOW CAN I BEST FULFILL THIS LIFE AND GET A SENSE OF MY GOD SELF? IF EVERYTHING IS SO ILLUSORY, WHY EXIST AT ALL?

A. I'll give you another *perception*. I was asked to make a deck of cards to help people remember Home. We called them "Key" cards, and there were to be 72 of them. I would go into the Akashic Records and ask to be shown Key card 1, 2 and so on. Source would show me the card, give me the image, and give me the name. And then I would describe it to AHONU, who would set about drawing it from my description. One of those cards was a clock called "The Moment." (AHONU, 2012) When I tuned into it, Source said that if we really understood The Moment, we would be in ecstasy all the time.

Source was saying "Can you imagine how wonderful it really is that you create an illusion of time so you could have any particular type of experience you desire and make it last for as long as you desire?"

The truth is that it's all for *experiencing*, and if you were experiencing from that frame of reference, it would all be ecstasy to you, because God *is* in every moment, no matter where you are. Since everything here is perception, even the perception that Source *isn't* here, or that you're not connected to it, is just a perception to be corrected.

Whatever you do, do it for the joy of doing it. There will come a time, however, when you will be done with perception and want to *be* your true Future Self, now.

You don't have to earn your way to Creator. You don't have to earn your way up the ladder. Part of what motivates people is they think they have to earn their way up the ladder. They do things or act in certain ways because they think it's going to get them somewhere, but actually *joy* is what everyone needs to remember and experience.

When you ask, "What can I do that would be the most benefit to my life?" the answer is, "Whatever you want." I know that's a nebulous answer—you probably wanted something more specific, but the truth is that you're free to do what you desire. If you perceive your life as lacking in any way, you can choose to have those lacks filled. You would have your own image of what that would look like.

As you begin to manifest those desires, your confidence will increase and you will gain confidence in your own sense of personal power. You will naturally want to experience "more"—to see what else you can manifest. Ultimately however, you will come to the place where there is never enough to fulfill you; no manifestation that will satisfy you indefinitely.

When you get to this place, you will begin to ask what *will* fulfill you and you will realize that only sharing love and *being* Love is the answer. Now your manifesting will have a different goal—it will be to feel and express love—to give and to love others. When you are done with the drama, and when you know how to love yourself and others, you will be ready to go

Home. You won't choose to "go Home" before this point, because your ego will always perceive of "going Home" as annihilation. So you can see why Source says to play in the illusion until you are really ready and why it is also saying to take your time with it.

Q. HOW DO I GET MORE IN TOUCH WITH THE TRUE REALITY OF WHO I AM AND BREAK FREE OF THE ILLUSION? TO KNOW WHAT MY PURPOSE IS?

A. First of all, we all have a contract because *we decided* on a contract. We *created* it. Even that isn't really a spiritual *necessity.* We created a contract as a way to have certain experiences that we think we'd like to have or need to have.

Your *"real self"* is listening to your desire to know the true reality and break free of the illusion, and it's saying "OK, *done.*" Now watch for the signs of it. It's that easy, if your desire is real. Don't worry about "how" the signs will come, just ask to be able to recognize them as they come.

The real question is, "Will you *allow* it?" If you say there are forces against you; it is really that you haven't allowed the experience to come. It isn't that the universe is saying "no" to any of your requests. Instead, there's a part of you that can't let yourself experience it. What I would really be asking of my real self is to help me be able to *allow* an experience of my real self, to receive the knowledge of my real self.

To be very honest, we have talked in the past about not being able to forgive ourselves; it's another way of explaining the above. As long as we can't forgive ourselves for the mistakes we *think* we've made in the past, we will not allow ourselves to experience something that will be very blissful and will erase our guilt. An experience of our *real self* is going to prove to us that we've never done anything wrong, and that no one else has either. We have to be ready to *allow* that to be, because that's what it's going to be.

If it were to show us that and give us evidence of it right now, we wouldn't even see it.

We've always been connected; we still are connected, and if we want to have an experience of it, we have to ask for help to be able to let go of all of the horrible things we *think* we've done, and anybody else who's done things to us. Self-judgment does not go with an experience of your real self. We have to give up one in order to experience the other. We've got to meet ourselves where we are.

Watch your mind and watch where you go with your ideas, thoughts, beliefs and emotions.

The idea of "karma" and "karmic lessons" are *experiences* that we set up based on our perceptions of what we think we need to do, or think we need to learn. The idea of "I have more work to do" is an idea made up by us. We've just explained that you don't have to earn anything.

With all of these experiences, ideas and illusions, you can see how it would be fun to say "I've got to get back and work really hard at that; I want to go back and accomplish being the best this or that—the best architect, the best doctor, the best healer, and the best teacher—I want to experience being that."

You can set up the drama and all the players will show up in your life to play their role in your play, which would also be *their* play, you know. On the one hand, Source would say, "Isn't that cool, look what you did!" And on the other hand Source doesn't care because It knows you have never left Home and have nothing to prove.

Q. DID WE CONTRACT TO COME HERE NOW TO BE TEACHERS OR HEALERS, BECAUSE WE UNDERSTAND THAT IN THIS ILLUSIONARY TIME CYCLE THERE'S ACCELERATED GROWTH HAPPENING AND THERE'S AN ACCELERATED OPPORTUNITY TO WAKE UP TO THE MEMORY OF OUR FUTURE SELF?

A. Yes, but it's still an illusion, because the Future Self that never left Home is outside of all that. But it is also a big stretch to actually say that we're all completely done with experiencing. I don't think very many are ready to do it. Surely, however, the influx of Light coming in will help us all awaken to the truth of what we've been speaking of here.

It would also be true that to be here now and receive this Light for awakening could be a soul contract for many of us. Some of us want off the wheel of karma and repeated lifetimes, but we perceive that as getting "out of" or "off of" Earth. We would be perfectly happy to leave Earth and never come back, but we assume that we will be having a life somewhere else—some other planet, for example. Those ideas are still in the realm of perception.

Q. HOW DOES A MAN WHO HAD MADE A VOW IN A PAST LIFE NOW RELEASE IT? HE ASKS HIS MASTER TEACHER, WHO SAYS, "YOU CAN'T BREAK A VOW LIKE THAT. NO WAY; IT WILL STAND LIFETIME AFTER LIFETIME, AND THAT'S IT." IS THIS TRULY THE WAY IT IS?

A. No! This is an unfortunate example of belief systems that are disempowering people. Source would say and remind us all that "at all times we are free." We will continue playing this game until we tire of it, but we will not tire of it until we get over our perception of lack, return to true prosperity, regain our personal power and remember our truth in love and our Home in God.

✤　✤　✤

The material you have just read is extremely thought-provoking and thus requires some additional comments. We began this book explaining that the questions are answered by Source at many different levels of awareness and understanding. This perspective is especially important in understanding the preceding material about our Future Selves.

The participants' focus of attention in their questions was on their next incarnation, but instead, Source replied from the perspective of the Big Picture—the all encompassing—and did not deal with the linear idea of lifetimes. Consequently, Source's responses could seem to suggest that our lives in this dimension, in other dimensions, and in the planes of existence after death are unnecessary and unimportant. Certainly one could conclude that the individuated spirit's journey to its God-realization and its soul "growth" through repeated incarnations is in the realm of illusion. In one sense (or level of awareness), it is illusory, but in another sense it isn't.

The foregoing material talks about our decision to return Home to a Self that has never left its Home in God—to a Self that is already God-realized. If so, then what is our journey all about? In the beginning chapters, we talked about the fall of Earth and discussed a digression into density in which our forms were eventually changed from spirit bodies to flesh bodies, from androgyny to gender divisions that resulted over eons in the loss of our spiritual memories. We spoke of the splitting of our spirits into two identities—a spirit body and a flesh body—and the ensuing inner conflict.

From this perspective, we can see that we are indeed on a journey to remembering who we are—a journey that is compromised by the karma we have created in our various lifetimes and by the continuing cycles of incarnations that result from that. The choices we make either accelerate or delay us on our journey. We must remember that our Self that is Home in God (our Future Self) is God Source's answer to any part of us that has fallen or forgotten, and the repair happened the moment our organic integrity was compromised. It is obvious that we, as human beings in dense physical bodies, have not realized that we have a Self that is creating with, and in, God Source and that our journey is intended to help us remember that we are spiritual extensions of God Source's Love.

The time it takes for us to arrive as our Future Selves will differ for each one of us, as we have been reincarnating for eons. It could happen in an instant, or it could take another millennium, depending on what choices we make throughout our lives, what we heal, forgive, release and remember. Surely, each and every moment of love brings us further into "true alignment" with our original selves.

Therefore, as we proceed in this lifetime and others, we need to expand our perceptions to see just how big the Big Picture is! It spans trillions of years—indeed time at that level may not even be within most people's capacity to understand. The decision to be finished with ego identities does not come overnight—it is a process that occurs naturally in the evolution of the spirit. So no fear need be involved, no worry or anxiety. The moment will occur for each of us in our own time.

Conclusion

We have found in our inquiry into this "Time of Change" that we are magnificent beings of Light that are, and always have been, back "Home" with our Creator. This part of us, the part that is still whole and intact, has called itself our "Future Self" because we have yet to "return" to it. We have been out of Home playing in time, space and dimensionality—having experiences and perceiving ourselves as separate from our Home. This perception gives us the ongoing drama of Earth changes, the negative agenda, karma, pain and suffering, *etc*.

As long as we feel or perceive that we are lacking, we will still desire to manifest experiences. As we do so, and we play with our personal power, we will find that our experiences aren't enough. Only then will we desire union with love and go from the desire to *get,* to the desire to *share*. Only then will we begin to return Home to our Future Selves.

A Time of Change is the first book in the Honest-to-God Series from the Akashic Records. Truly we have only touched the surface, and as we continue on into *The Nature of Reality,* the second book in the series, we discuss topics like Time and Dimensions, Miracles, Gravity, Death and Near-Death Experiences, God/Creator, Twin Flames and Soul Mates, UFOs and ETs, Crop Circles, Advanced Children and more.

We hope you will join us on our continuing journey through the Akashic Records!

The Nature of Reality is scheduled to be released in April, 2013.

Symbolism in Your Everyday Life

This article is for those of you who are interested in increasing your daily awareness of the symbolism in your 3-D life and how it relates to what you are creating beneath the level of your conscious awareness. This symbolism is the direct result of the *process of association* that you make within yourself by the belief patterns and experiences of your life. It is how you, as an individual, interpret what you had been taught or what you have experienced—the emotional and mental impact, the "conclusions" you come to.

In the creative field of association beneath the surface of your conscious awareness, your interpretation of reality combines with the life force energy moving in and through us at all times, and congeals into a "manifestation," "occurrence," "situation," "relationship," *etc.* There is no judgment in this process—it is just the fact of how the Law of Cause and Effect works.

It is much like the process of dreaming. We can understand that when we dream, our consciousness is "acting out" its different perceptions and associations of the day, week, or events. Much the same is true in the experiences of our 3-D world. As the final "stage" of our consciousness, the 3-D landscape is a dreamscape—it is the culmination point of our perceptions, learning, opinions, and most importantly, our choices. In each moment we are given the opportunity to see not only the content and condition of our consciousness, but how the choices are based upon the associative symbolism contained within our own subconscious minds.

The *Language of Symbolism* can be both literal and symbolic. Names, places, events, all tell a story about where we are on all four levels—physical, emotional, mental, and spiritual. They are also reflections of what we believe to be true about reality and "our" reality. In actuality, consciousness is free. This means it is the one thing that remains true through every event, relationship, and circumstance. The "us" that is the perceiver is running the show. It is the "us" that sees, experiences, associates, and decides. Consciousness then "reflects" this as a story being acted out on the 3-D screen of our lives.

As it is being "displayed externally," we can modify or change the scene by being aware and observing the "content" of the reflection—what it is saying or symbolizing as the reflector of our consciousness. This becomes quite an exciting and fun exercise once you get the hang of it!

The quality of the 3-D story is always a symbolic out-picturing of our individual and collective consciousness. Learning to examine what your "out-picture" or manifestation is showing you is the art of conscious dreaming and the journey of freedom.

It has been my experience that this practice leads you to conscious, active participation and choice in your everyday world. It gives you the ability to say "Yes, I accept this version of my reality," or "No, I do not accept this. I choose instead…" This must be done with a firm and deliberate decision.

The effectiveness of this process is determined by your certainty of knowing that in each moment, because you said so, the Law of Creation says "Yes, OK, whatever you say."

This Law does not decide for you if your choices or decisions are healthy or unhealthy, productive or counterproductive—it just says, "*Yes!*" There is enormous freedom in this fact, if you can embrace it. It means that at all times *you* are in charge of your external hologram, your individual dreamscape.

At all times, *you* are the decider of how you will interpret or see events and experiences; *you* determine whether it's heaven or hell for you or something in between; you build your own progress and evolution by the decisions you make internally and consciously.

The fun part of this process (it's all fun, actually!) is looking at the symbolism that's in your own life. Taking a look at this also tells you what your choices are in your *now* moment. This needs to be said - if you are looking at your 3-D landscape and not liking what you are seeing or creating, it is not too late to make it different. *You are always in your moment of power,* as that is the only place you can be. Your power is operating all the time, whether you are a conscious creator or an unconscious one. This is the Law of Creation—it says "*yes*" to whatever we think, believe, perceive, and makes more of it. When you *change your mind* or decide anew, it will say "*yes*" to that too!

TIMING

This is an area where people have the biggest issue. They want to know "why" their manifestations take "time." Actually, some take only a minute to change; others take days, some weeks, months, or years. Why is that? My personal experience tells me it is "belief and action dependent." What I mean by this is that the clearer, more deliberate, more certain someone is that "because they said so it *will be!*" the more quickly things seem to manifest.

We dilute our creations by being unaware of programmed beliefs that say *how* something can be done—such as "It takes time," "I have to do it this way," "I have to earn this," "I need a degree," "There's too much competition," "It's too hard," "It takes effort," "No pain, no gain," "I didn't do anything to deserve this," "Others will think I'm crazy," "What if...," *etc.* I could go on forever with the litany of "why it can't be done."

We all have these programs—it is in the mass consciousness of the entire world. It is important and *necessary* to explore your own programs —or fears about change. If you do so, you can learn to laugh at them and decide to believe otherwise. This process works with *word* associations also. You can change the *definition* of any word that has a limiting or negative association for you. Just *redefine* it to mean something fun, joyful, and productive!

Trigger words can be: responsibility, work, relationships, marriage, commitment, money, exercise, love, diet, career, authority, government, laws, rules, school, education, learning, religion, parents, sex, jobs, to name a few.

You may have your own set of words with which you associate limitations. Whatever they may be, sit down and write your perceived definitions of them, and then redefine them to be something productive, joyful, free and positive. Just doing the above exercise will begin a transformation process within your reality. Keep a journal for these purposes.

As you get proficient with this, the *time* element between when you decide differently and its *appearance* in your 3-D reality begins to collapse. What can you embody and accept? What can you actually integrate into your life? How far can you go? Where do your limiting concepts stop you in your tracks or thwart your ability to *imagine*?

When you *do* create a different reality, how well can you go with it and change? What changes will it cause in your life that you need to be willing to adjust to? How flexible are you? And remember also that there is no *ultimate* end.

After each manifesting accomplishment, there comes a time when it will no longer satisfy, and you will desire to grow further and expand. This is normal, as you will transition from "things" to "qualities," and you will desire to reach higher and more expanded states of being. You will find yourself having this be the focus of your desires. You will find yourself walking right into the heart of Divine Love and gratitude.

Be especially conscious in your creations that you respect the free will of others—it is not OK to project your will on specific people or specific situations without another's consent! Remember—*like attracts to itself that which it is*—that is all you need to know!

Here is an example of making the connection between your outer and inner life:

A couple I know recently bought an older house as an investment. It needed some fixing up before they could resell it. One of the problems was that the floor had settled from age and was uneven in places. It was stable, just uneven.

As the husband was jacking up the *supporting beam* under the house, the cinder blocks suddenly disintegrated. Being a conscious creator, the husband knew that symbolically he was being shown that the *foundation* needed something much stronger than it had been built on in the past (as in the "foundation" for his life, his wife's life, their future, *etc.*). Both decided to consciously be responsible for creating a stronger foundation in every way that was required.

As the week progressed they were out looking for other real estate one day and saw a lumber yard. They decided to stop by to see what there was that could be used as a *stronger support* for under their house. The husband would have been content with a thick piece of

pine, but the workman said, "No, I have just the thing." He pro-
ceeded to bring out 2 thick pieces of *oak* "And it is *no charge!*"

The couple laughed at the symbolism of this because they knew
they were "twin flames" who have twin oak trees as the symbol for
their relationship!

Another investor couple I know had the opportunity to buy an old *his-
toric* house that needed a lot of work. There was no kitchen or heating system. The husband knew that if the house were *brought back to its original
glory*, it would be worth a lot of money and he would enjoy *restoring* it. (In
this case, the house symbolized the husband wanting to recover something
from his past that he had lost). The problem here was that the down pay-
ment on this house would have taken all the couple's resources, leaving
them with no money for living or repairs. It seemed that the *cost* for going
back and fixing the past would be very high.

How necessary is this? The situation was showing the unhealed part of
the man, and his desire to recover a former life. What are the *choices* in this
situation? After seeing the symbolic implications of this house, the couple
decided to let the house go in favor of something more modern and less
costly. They realized the futility of hanging onto the past, and made a commitment to the *now* and to a *new* future. It is as easy as this.

In the universe, either choice would have been OK to make—but one
was obviously more struggle oriented. It was just as easy to say, "*No*, I want
my *now* and my *future* to be easier and newer." They soon found another
house that served them in their new purpose.

Take a look around you now and examine what you are seeing in your
reality. What is the *content* of your daily life? Has the same thing been
going on for a while now? What is the pattern or association you are seeing
manifest?

You can do this practice with your sleeping dreams as well—all are
symbols from the unconscious playing themselves out in a drama. What
would you like to change or be different? Where or what are your limiting
perceptions that tell you that *you can't*? Consider your waking reality as the

dreamscape that it is and have fun exploring the movie and what it *means* to you.

In this time of change, the *ask and you shall receive* potential has quickened to the point of almost instant manifestation. This is true on every level of existence so that any problem you may be having can reveal a solution immediately.

Put yourself in conscious choosing, and remember: who you are is unlimited potential!

About the Author

AINGEAL ROSE O'GRADY

Aingeal Rose's spiritual journey began after the tragic death of her first husband just three months after their wedding day. She dedicated herself to finding the answers to the deepest spiritual questions, journeying into the mysteries of the Spirit world, exploring consciousness and its expansive potential.

She held a private practice in Chicago for over 20 years and since 2007 expanded her practice throughout the United States and Ireland. She has transformed the lives of countless people through her workshops and classes in Manifesting and Self-Healing, Exploring the Planes of Existence After Death, Beginner through Advanced TAROT, Healing Spreads and more. Aingeal Rose has worked with whales and dolphins, sacred sites, sacred geometry, planetary physics, and the 2012 personal ascension process.

She holds certifications in Psychic Laser Therapy, Kathara Healing, Soul Retrieval, Reiki, Cellular Re-patterning, and reading the Akashic Records. She also makes one-of-a-kind Handmade Fairies for customers around the globe. She reads the Akashic Records privately for clients' worldwide and is widely known for her Group Akashic Records sessions as presented in this book.

As a seasoned spiritual teacher, she has helped her students and clients achieve greater personal growth and self-mastery through self-honesty and humor. She is the author of *Tarot for Beginners* and can be contacted from her website at: http://aingealrose.com.

Bibliography

- *Matthew 7:6*

- ECCH (2009). *The Legal Situation for the Practice of Homeopathy in Europe.* Retrieved from Scribd: http://tinyurl.com/9s3qr48

- AHONU (2012). *AHONU Visionary Artist.* Retrieved from: http://ahonu.com

- Chaitow, Leon (2004). *Vaccination and Immunization: Dangers, Delusions and Alternatives (What every parent should know).* ISBN 978-0852071915. Published by C.W. Daniel.

- FDA (2009). *FDA Food Labeling Guide.* Retrieved from Food and Drug Administration (FDA): http://tinyurl.com/nje6mh

- Observer (2011). *The Leitrim Observer Archives.* Retrieved from The Leitrim Observer Newspaper: http://tinyurl.com/8mnkxwx

- PSRAST (1

- 999). *Genetically Engineered Food—Safety Problems.* Retrieved from Physicians and Scientists for Responsible Application of Science and Technology http://tinyurl.com/9pcrv3u

- Technology (2009). *Food Matters.tv.* Retrieved from http://tinyurl.com/7jxzl4l

- Times (2011). *The Irish Times Archive.* Retrieved from The Irish Times.com: http://tinyurl.com/9m5ysjl

- Wellness (2012). *In the News.* Retrieved from Arche Wellness: http://tinyurl.com/d9rff4m

- WHO (2012). *WHO Food Safety.* Retrieved from WHO: http://tinyurl.com/4q5ne

- Wikipedia (2011). *Men in Black.* Retrieved from Wikipedia: http://tinyurl.com/nunug

- Wikipedia. (2012, April 14). *Samuel Hahnemann—Founder of Homeopathy.* Retrieved from Wikipedia: http://tinyurl.com/27572n

Appendix

SUICIDES

In Ireland alone in 2011 there were over 536 suicides, the highest in its history (Times, 2011), and that was people of all ages. A study compared data from 1993-1998 and 2003 to 2008 and found that the suicide rate for children and teenagers has doubled in Ireland since 1993 and the same study also found there was a 40 percent increase in the rate of suicide among boys aged 15 to 17 since 1993, with the number of girls under 18 taking their own lives doubling during the same period (Observer, 2011).

You do need to be aware of the negative agenda (NA) because they know the technology now of electromagnetic pulsing. They know how to alter your brain waves. So be aware, eat well, rest and stay well hydrated. Also keep your food pure and avoid genetically modified (GMO) foods. Take care of yourself, because you're going to need your powers of discernment.

HOMEOPATHY

The first Homeopathic hospital was in Philadelphia, PA in the U.S. It was named after Samuel Hahnemann, the founder of Homeopathy. It has since been turned into an all allopathic hospital. Samuel Hahnemann himself went there for treatment in his later years when he was dying and found there were NO remaining Homeopathic doctors there to help him (Wikipedia, Samuel Hahnemann - Founder of Homeopathy, 2012)

FOOD LABELING

Always read the labels on the foods you buy. No matter what the front of the box or package says, always turn it over and read the ingredients section carefully! Natural does *not* mean organic.

Many products no longer show where they were made but only give where the distributor is located. With much of our food and pet products now coming from overseas, it is best to make sure you read the labels at the store when buying food products. It is our right to know the country of origin and what our food contains. (FDA, 2009).

The U.S. Food & Drug Administration mandates country-of-origin labeling on many food products, but there are exceptions, most notably the entire category of "processed foods." (FDA, 2009). Consumer groups are currently advocating the closure of these loopholes.

Discerning the country of origin from the barcode can be misleading and unreliable, on two counts:

There's more than one kind of bar code in use around the world. UPC bar codes, the type most commonly used in the United States, do not typically contain a country identifier. A different type of bar code known as EAN-13 does contain a country identifier, but it's more commonly used in Europe and other countries outside the U.S.

Even in the case of EAN-13 bar codes, the digits associated with country of origin don't necessarily specify where the product was manufactured, but rather where the bar code itself was registered. So, for example, a product manufactured in China and sold in France could have an EAN-13 bar code identifying it as a "French" product.

If a Mexican company imported fruit from Guatemala, then packed and shipped that fruit to the United States, the country code portion of the final product's bar code would likely indicate an origin of Mexico rather than Guatemala. It may be the case that in some parts of the world there is a fair degree of correlation between assignment of bar codes and product origins (i.e., in some countries the preponderance of bar code assignments may apply to domestic products), but for surefire product origin identification consumers must rely upon other methods. In determining the country of origin of a product sold in the U.S., consumers should still look for "Made in [country name]" labels on the packaging.

GM FOOD LABELING

In 1992, the FDA declared that biotech foods were the same as conventional foods. (PSRAST, 1999) Unless the label specifically states "certified organic," it is a safe bet that any food containing corn, soy, and cottonseed oils has a GMO origin. These processed foods will not have the genetically engineered PLU code that would alert the consumer. In addition, manufacturers of GMO products are not subjected to any special review, approval, or labeling. The organic producer is, however. Ironic, isn't it - something that is grown naturally requires more scrutiny than does something containing any number of harmful substances?

(See "Q. What about genetically modified food?" on page 55.)

ORGANIC LABELING

Before a product can be labeled organic, stringent guidelines must be followed. Producers must have had their farms inspected and be given permission to use the "certified organic" label on their product. Organic farmers try their best to make sure their seed has not been contaminated through cross-pollination and go to their own great expense to do so. The onus of a pure product is placed squarely on the shoulders of the organic grower, and his efforts should be acknowledged and supported.

The following labeling guidelines are according to The National Organic Program, which prohibits the use of antibiotics, growth hormones, chemical insecticides, herbicides, fungicides, and fertilizers in organic dairy, meat, and poultry. In addition, farmers must use organic seed and feed.

However, changes in these standards, made in April 2004, expand the use of antibiotics and hormones in organic dairy cows, allow more pesticides, and for the first time, permit organic livestock to eat potentially contaminated fishmeal. Relaxing of the following standards makes it even more important to buy from a local organic farmer that you know.

"100% Organic" or "Certified Organic" means that all of the substances, ingredients, processing aids, food additives, including colors and flavors, are certified organic.

Organic" means that only 95% of the ingredients must be organic, leaving the remaining 5% open to "allowable" substances from the USDA's National List of Allowed Substances and include such things as:

- Synthetic substances allowed in organic crop production.
- Synthetic inert ingredients as classified by the EPA for use with non-synthetic substances or synthetic substances used as allowed crop or livestock pesticide ingredients.
- Non-synthetic substances prohibited for use in organic crop, livestock production and processing.
- Synthetic substances allowed for use in organic livestock production.
- Nonagricultural (non-organic) (both non-synthetic and synthetic) substances allowed as ingredients in or on processed products labeled as "organic" or "made with organic (specified ingredients or food group(s)."
- Non-organically produced agricultural products allowed as ingredients in or on processed products labeled as organic or made with organic ingredients.

"Made with organic ingredients" means that only 70% of the ingredients have to be organic. The other 30% contain non-organic ingredients and synthetic substances normally allowed in conventional food and fiber production. Products with less than 70% organic ingredients have to list only the organic ingredients on the ingredient panel rather than the primary panel.

In addition, foods that come from abroad are irradiated, organic or not.

VACCINATIONS

The following information is just a sample of what is available for exploration. The information covers the history of vaccinations and shows that the reason many illnesses, such as polio, cleared up was because of improved sanitation conditions and not the vaccines.

Dr. Viera Scheibner was a leading researcher in the anti-vaccination field and has been writing and lecturing about vaccinations since her study in the 1980s of babies' stress-induced breathing patterns introduced her to the subject and led her to collect and study more than 100,000 pages of medical papers on vaccination. For more information, visit her website: http://vierascheibner.org.

Another book by Leon Chaitow (2004) *Vaccination and Immunization: Dangers, Delusions and Alternatives (What every parent should know)* is an easily read book on the topic. ISBN 978-0852071915. Published by C.W. Daniel.

MEN IN BLACK

Men in Black (MIB) in American popular culture and in UFO conspiracy theories are men dressed in black suits who claim to be government agents who harass or threaten UFO witnesses to keep them quiet about what they have seen. It is sometimes implied that they may be aliens themselves. The term is also frequently used to describe mysterious men working for unknown organizations, as well as to various branches of government allegedly designed to protect secrets or perform other strange activities. The term is generic, used for any unusual, threatening or strangely behaved individual whose appearance on the scene can be linked in some fashion with UFO sightings (Wikipedia, Men in Black, 2011).

Index

Wild Flower Press
        Imprint of Granite Publishing L.L.C.
P.O. Box 1429
Columbus, NC 28722

http://granite-planet.net

Look for
Volume II in the
Honest-To-God Series

The Nature of Reality:
Akashic Guidance for
Understanding Life and Its Purpose

publishing in April 2013

Aingeal Rose O'Grady

http://aingealrose.com

16439867R00106

Made in the USA
Charleston, SC
20 December 2012